Munjed Al Muderis: From Refugee To Surgical Inventor

Aussie STEM Stars

Story Told By Dianne Wolfer

16pt

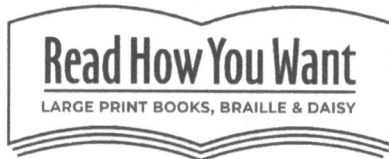

Read How You Want
LARGE PRINT BOOKS, BRAILLE & DAISY

Copyright Page from the Original Book

Aussie STEM Stars series
Published by Wild Dingo Press
Melbourne, Australia
books@wilddingopress.com.au
wilddingopress.com.au

This work was first published by Wild Dingo Press 2020
Text copyright © Dianne Wolfer

The moral right of the author has been asserted.

Cover Design: Gisela Beer
Illustrations: Diana Silkina
Series Editor: Catherine Lewis
Printed in Australia

Wolfer, Dianne 1961-, author.
Munjed Al Muderis: From refugee to surgical inventor / Dianne Wolfer

A catalogue record for this
book is available from the
National Library of Australia

TABLE OF CONTENTS

1: 1980: War begins   1

2: 1981: Young entrepreneur   18

3: Baghdad chessboard   31

4: 1989/91: Bullies, bombs and books   43

5: 1999: First, do no harm   61

6: 1999: Fleeing for his life...   73

7: Nowhere to go   84

8: High seas without a skipper   92

9: You are not welcome   106

10: 1999/2000: #982   119

11: Still waiting   130

12: 2001: Survival of the fittest   145

13: 'I'll be back'   157

Glossary   171

About Dianne Wolfer   174

Disclaimer

This work has been developed in collaboration with Associate Professor Munjed Al Muderis. The utmost care has been taken to respectfully portray, as accurately as memory allows, the events and the stories of all who appear in this work. The publishers assume no liability or responsibility for unintended inaccuracies, but would be pleased to rectify at the earliest opportunity any omissions or errors brought to their notice.

1

1980: War begins

'We must fly home immediately.'
'Why?' Munjed asks his father.
'Saddam Hussein has invaded Iran.'
Munjed is only eight but he knows that Saddam Hussein is the president of their country, Iraq.
'Why?' he asks again.
'Munjed, do as your father says!'
His mother, Kamila, has just returned from the supermarket and Munjed knows better than to argue when she uses that tone of voice. He frowns instead. The Detroit hotel where they're staying has a great games' area and there are plenty of kids his age.

Munjed doesn't want their summer holiday to end.

His mother drops her bag on the counter with the groceries, smooths her floral dress and turns to her husband.

'It may not be safe to return to Baghdad,' she says, quietly.

'We must go back while we can.'

'I think we should stay here.'

The atmosphere in the room is tense. Munjed tries to make himself invisible as his parents discuss the situation in their country and what they should do.

Finally, his father whispers, 'I am an Iraqi. I should die at home in my own country.'

Baba is an affectionate term for Dad in many languages including Arabic which is spoken in Iraq.

For once his mother has no reply.

'Are you sick, *Baba?*' Munjed asks, forgetting to be invisible.

His father laughs and opens his arms.

'No, my son, but we must return. I can't leave my homeland when there is conflict.'

Abdul Razak Al Muderis is a Supreme Court judge. He's a soft-spoken academic, a natural leader with a strong sense of social justice. Through Abdul, Munjed can trace his ancestry to one of the nine traditional rulers of Baghdad and also to the Prophet Muhammad who is the prophet all Muslims follow.

Munjed sits with his father until his mother calls him.

'Come and help me pack.'

'Why are we in such a rush?' Munjed complains.

His mother pushes loose hair behind her ears. 'Iranian planes will target Baghdad Airport. We need to arrive before they do.'

Kamila has worked as a teacher and school principal. She's tough and practical, traits that will help her save her son's life in later years when he flees Iraq to find safety in a new homeland.

'Don't worry,' she says, ruffling Munjed's hair. 'Everything will be fine.'

Although her voice is calm, Kamila's eyes are anxious. An unfamiliar feeling of dread settles in Munjed's stomach as the Al Muderis family zip their suitcases and hail a taxi.

'The airport,' his father tells the driver. 'Please hurry.'

The KLM Airlines desk is already crowded.

'We need to catch the next flight to Baghdad,' Abdul tells the clerk.

'Yes, sir.' The man checks his screen. 'The best connection is via Athens. It leaves in a few hours.'

Before they board, Abdul listens to the latest news broadcast. The conflict in Iraq is worsening. Ever since Munjed can remember, his family have spent summer holidays abroad. This is the only time they've returned early.

The aeroplane is a 747 jumbo. Munjed settles into his seat. It's a long flight but they're in business class so the seats are comfortable.

'Would you like another bowl of ice cream?' a steward asks. Munjed nods.

He loves the free colouring-in books the stewards give him, best of all is the miniature aeroplane model they bring.

Munjed zooms the plane around the seats then makes a careful landing on his tray table.

Eleven hours later, their flight arrives in Athens and the Al Muderis family connect with their eight-hour flight to Baghdad. As Munjed drifts off to sleep, he wonders what's happening at home and whether his best friends, Manaf and Ayser, are safe.

'Excuse me, passengers.' A crackly noise wakes him. It's mid-flight. The pilot is making an announcement over the PA. 'I'm sorry to interrupt your rest, but we've just learnt that Baghdad Airport is closed to all non-military aircraft. This flight is now being diverted to Amman in Jordan. KLM Royal Dutch Airlines apologises for any inconvenience.'

Munjed feels his stomach drop as the plane dips then turns sharply. The woman behind him screams and people shout questions.

'What's going on?'

'Is Baghdad being bombed?'

'Will it be safe to land in Jordan?'

Munjed's parents exchange worried glances.

'We might have to take a bus from Amman,' Abdul whispers.

'That will take ages,' Kamila says.

'It's the only way...'

His mother grips Munjed's hand and says, 'It will be fine'. The high pitch of her voice frightens him even more.

At Amman's Queen Alia Airport, his father takes charge again.

'Are there any flights at all to Baghdad?' he asks the frazzled Jordanian clerk.

'I'm sorry, sir, there's no civilian air access into Iraq.'

'But we must return home.'

'The only way into Baghdad is by road,' the clerk replies, 'however, that could be dangerous. I don't recommend it.'

As Munjed's father makes arrangements to catch a bus, his mother gathers three chairs.

'Come,' she says. 'Let's try and rest.'

It's impossible to sleep on the drooping, plastic chairs. Munjed wanders around, watching other travellers and reading notices. The building is little more than a shed. He learns that the ramshackle airport is named after a queen who died in a helicopter accident a few years earlier.

That doesn't make him feel safer.

They spend all night in the terminal. The hours pass slowly. Munjed pokes spider webs and watches moths scorch themselves on a dusty light. He has never been so bored.

'What's happening at home?' Munjed asks his parents.

'Stop worrying,' his mother replies. 'Everything will be alright.'

His father adds, 'Only that which is meant to happen, will happen'.

They wait in the airport for 19 hours, trying to rest as best they can in the uncomfortable chairs. When at last their transport arrives, things become even worse. The Iraqi Airways bus looks ancient. Its lights are so dim that Munjed can barely see it rumble towards them.

> **Q:** Can pinching your nose really help you feel calmer?
>
> **A:** Yes, breathing through alternate nostrils helps sharpen your concentration by allowing equal amounts of oxygen to both sides of

your brain. **Alternate nostril breathing** is a good thing to do before an important event when you need to think clearly.

Another medical technique Munjed uses to calm his nervous system during challenging moments is massaging his ear lobes.

'Why are the headlights covered in blue paint?' he asks.

'Less light,' the driver mutters. 'We don't want Iranian bombers to see us.'

Munjed swallows, imagining fighter planes swooping at them. His father is the wisest person he knows, but surely this is a mistake. They climb onto the bus with other travellers from their flight and sit on rough bench seats. At dusk they begin the torturous overnight journey to Iraq. Military aircraft scream through the skies and Munjed asks his mother whether their home in Baghdad is being attacked.

'All will be well,' she soothes.

Everything is dark. There are no streetlights and the bus headlights are too faint for Munjed to see the road ahead. He hopes the driver has good eyesight because he's driving very fast. Vehicles are travelling in both directions. Their headlights are also painted blue. Munjed shivers. He knows that pinching his nose and breathing through separate nostrils is a good way to calm his nerves. As they bounce over the pot-holed road, he does this during the most terrifying moments.

The bus stops at Trebil on the Iraqi-Jordanian border. The Al Muderis family get off and stretch their legs.

'Passports, please.'

Stern-faced officials inspect their documents.

Stamp, stamp, stamp. They're waved on.

Munjed's stomach grumbles. His mother wants to buy some bread and water, but there are no shops at the desert checkpoint.

'Everyone back on the bus,' the driver calls. Even he looks anxious now.

Once they enter Iraq the highways are wide and smooth. One thing Saddam Hussein's regime does well is road building. As they drive closer to the Euphrates River, the landscape becomes greener because Saddam has introduced a law that every household must plant an olive tree. Otherwise they will be fined.

Near the town of Ramadi, about 100 kilometres before Baghdad, Munjed sees tree-lined villages. He sighs with relief. They're nearly home. Finally, they reach the outskirts of the capital. But it's all dark and shadowy – no one wants to attract the attention of Iranian bombers.

The Al Muderis home is also in complete darkness when they arrive, and their housekeeper welcomes the family with worried eyes.

'Why do the windows have duct-tape crosses?' Munjed asks her, although he guesses the answer before she can reply.

'If the house is bombed only part of the glass pane will shatter.'

After their exhausting journey across half the world, the family are desperate for a restful night. But no sooner has Munjed collapsed into bed, than he hears the deafening wail of an air-raid siren. They all run to shelter in the bathroom where the walls are the sturdiest. Being crammed in this small room together feels horrible.

From the bathroom's high window they watch the night sky explode as an eerie dome of antiaircraft fire spatters the darkness. Every tenth shot is a fiery red indicator, like the eyes of a furious dragon winking in the heavens.

For two weeks Baghdad is pounded. Iraq's antiaircraft guns return fire with a booming **ack-ackack.** Bombs land close to their home, sometimes within one kilometre. Other houses are damaged, but the Al Muderis family is lucky. Munjed worries for their neighbours and shudders each time a nearby street is hit. Their windows finally shatter when a massive bomb lands on a double-storey freeway just over a kilometre away. The concrete slabs collapse and Munjed hopes no one was driving on the freeway.

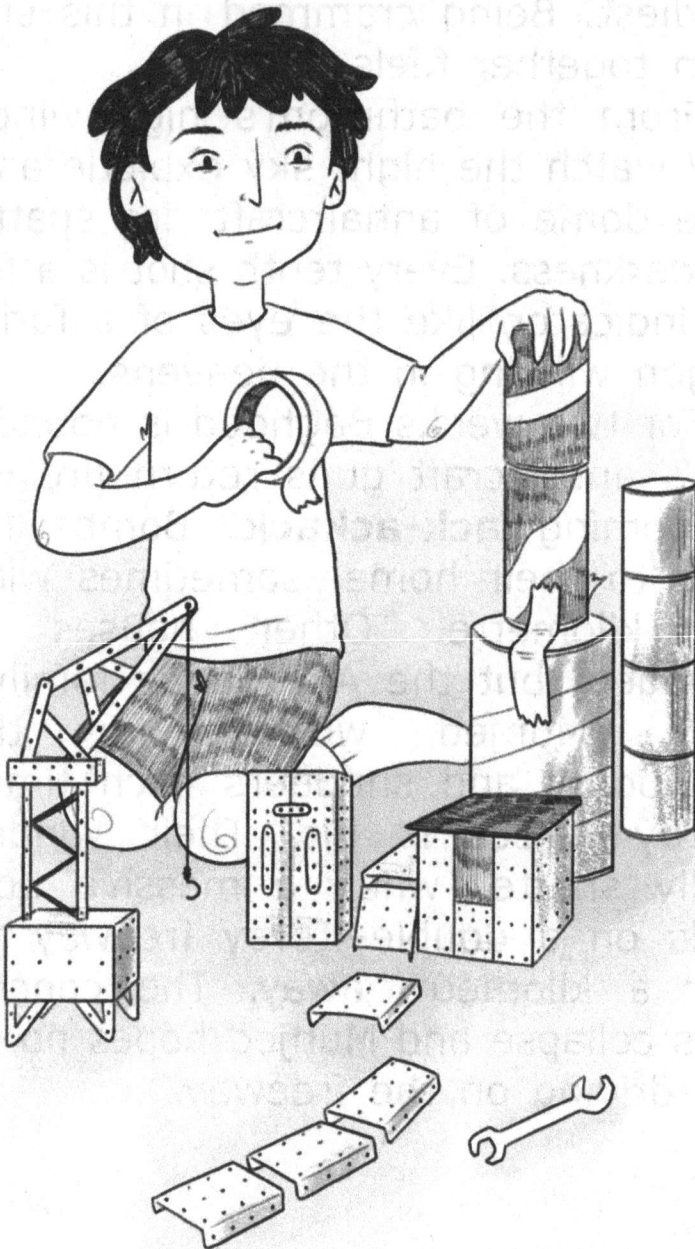

The Al Muderis radio stays tuned to the emergency channel to hear when an air raid is imminent. The announcer always says, 'Al Waleed is approaching you'. That's code for 'an air raid is close'. The rest of the time the station plays patriotic music.

When the warning is made, they rush to turn off lights and huddle in the bathroom, or under the stairs. As fighter jets roar overhead dropping missiles, they light candles. Munjed's mother chats to the servants, trying to calm them and his father opens a book and reads by the soft light. His steady voice makes Munjed feel safe.

When the danger has passed, the radio voice says, 'We hand you over the olive branches'. That's another code phrase meaning 'the skies are clear'. They sigh with relief and leave their cramped bolthole. They've survived another bombing raid!

At the beginning of the war, before the Iraqi pilots push back, Iranian aircraft dominate the skies so it isn't safe to be outside. Stuck in the house all day, Munjed spends his time tinkering with Meccano. He's building a city in his bedroom with skyscrapers made from empty tins linked to Meccano infrastructure. Tape holds the buildings in place and roads snake between them. Munjed thinks it's his best ever metropolis, but his mother and housekeeper are tired of stepping around it. Clearly, they don't appreciate his genius.

'This is ridiculous,' his mother complains. 'Your room must be cleaned. Anything could be hiding under those towers...'

Munjed shakes his head. 'It's taken me days to make. I'm not ready to pull it down!' The bombs have made everyone jittery and Munjed knows his reply is testing his mother's patience, but he's confident that his father will support him. Abdul Razak encourages anything that stimulates the brain and sparks creativity. As his mother grumbles, Munjed remembers another time years earlier, when he was just as defiant. Little Munjed had a creative mind and he decided to use crayons to redecorate his bedroom wall. His mother was furious. She'd pulled him by the ear and marched him to his father.

'Look what your son has done to the wall,' she scolded.

'Why did you do this?' his father asked him.

'I don't like the colour of my room.'

'Picasso says that, "every child is an artist",' Abdul reminded Kamila. 'Let the boy finish his task.'

Picasso was a famous Spanish artist who lived from 1881-1973.

His mother frowned, but accepted the decision.

There was no ladder and little Munjed could only reach a third of the way up the wall. He had a handful of crayons which soon became worn down stubs. By the time he was finished, his wall looked like an ugly, brown river of mud.

He'd worked hard, but instead of improving his bedroom, he'd made a horrible mess. That day Munjed learnt a valuable lesson, one that he's never forgotten: it's better to be prepared than to rush in quickly and fail.

That's one of the things Munjed loves most about his father – the way he encourages Munjed to discover things for himself. Abdul has taught him that it's okay to fail. Failing is another way to learn.

As the war continues, Munjed remembers this lesson and works more carefully on his metropolis. With unlimited Meccano, Munjed's skyscrapers grow taller until at last, even he becomes tired of them. To his mother's relief he eventually dismantles the city and builds a huge robot instead. Attaching arms to the robot's torso is fiddly, it needs a steady hand. But Munjed comes from a family of doctors and he has already decided to be a surgeon. Constructing a metal robot is good practice.

He tightens the last bolt and calls his father.

'Look,' Munjed says proudly. 'It's finished.'

His father smiles: 'Through patience, great things are accomplished'.

A sudden explosion startles them. It's another surface-to-air missile (SAM). His mother dims the lights, and while his father keeps on reading by candlelight, Munjed peers out a window. He scans the sky as Iranian planes drop bombs haphazardly. Then he turns back to his robot, rearranges its legs and builds a jet. Munjed's Meccano plane attacks his robot but that soon becomes boring. There are real-life fighter jets outside the window. He watches them instead.

2

1981: Young entrepreneur

Munjed is only eight but he has big plans.

'*Baba,* a quarter of a dinar is not enough pocket money,' he complains to his father.

'A quarter of a dinar is plenty,' Abdul replies.

'But Manaf's father gives him much more every week—'

'You should think of ways to earn your money properly.'

Munjed frowns. What can he do to increase his income? There must be something. He soon comes up with a plan. It's brilliant.

He will go into business. Iraqis love snacking on sunflower seeds. This gives Munjed a bright idea. He borrows money from his mother, then asks his father's driver to take him to a nearby market where he buys a huge bag of seeds.

Back home, he flavours them with unusual spices and roasts them. They smell delicious. When they've cooled, he sells them door-to-door around the neighbourhood. Although Munjed's business does well, he soon has an even better idea.

Iraqis also love kite fighting. The local kids all own small kites with sharp attachments tied to their single-line strings. They challenge each other to airborne battles. The aim is to cut the line of the other kite and win.

Munjed sets to work designing paper kites out of old newspaper. His kites have a palm frond down the middle as a shaft and everything is held together with sticky tape. None of that is unusual but his creations have a secret element. It's all in the string he uses.

After a lot of experimenting, Munjed perfects a fearsome coating for his kite strings. He crushes old light bulbs, grinds the glass and mixes it with glue. Then he pastes the sharp concoction over the string. It's difficult to see the fine glass coating on the string but it easily slices the strings of other kites. His creations become super popular. Best of all, no one discovers his secret ingredient.

The war drags on. Between attacks, Munjed goes to primary school with his two best friends, Ayser and Manaf. The friends come from very different families. Ayser's parents are strict and religious and follow the Shi'ite sect of Islam, while Manaf's family are Sunnis but are not overly devout. Manaf's mum works at Munjed's school and his dad is a senior police officer.

Differences between **Shi'a** and **Sunni** Muslims are similar to different sects or denominations in other religions. They believe in the same prophet of that religion, but have some different beliefs about how to live and pray and even dress.

In Ayser's family, visitors are not welcome after six in the evening, when their door is closed. So the boys always get together at either Munjed's or Manaf's place.

For the three friends, religious differences don't matter. Who cares which religion or sect their parents follow? Unfortunately, the leaders of their country and countries that neighbour Iraq are less open-minded.

During the war years, Munjed's Uncle Salman and Aunt Nuhad come to stay because their home in Basra, on the southern border, is being pounded by Iranian artillery. Much of Basra has become rubble. The bombing is indiscriminate. Schools, hospitals and houses are flattened. Munjed's aunt and uncle are both teachers, and the schools aren't safe. They take refuge in Baghdad where the bombing is less intense.

One day when the air-raid siren blares, Munjed and his uncle rush outside to watch the action. An exciting dogfight between Iraqi and Iranian aircraft is happening in the sky above them.

'Look at that!'

'Yes, and over there...'

They stand in the driveway craning their necks. Salman swings young Munjed onto his shoulders so he'll have a better view. Suddenly an Iranian Phantom fighter plane leaves the battle. It hurtles towards them, firing rockets in a spectacular display. Munjed and his uncle are mesmerised.

They stare as the pilot flies closer, closer, closer. Suddenly the fighter jet is strafing the ground immediately ahead of them. Bullets tear the grass. The earth explodes. Munjed's terrified uncle is frozen to the spot. Bullets hit the driveway, so close that Munjed and his uncle could easily be killed. They whistle past Munjed's head and slam into the house. Uncle Salman is *still* unable to move. The fighter jet turns to fly home but is shot down by an anti-aircraft missile.

As flames consume the plane, his mother races out. Her fury is as fierce as any jet fire.

'How can you be so stupid?' she screeches at his uncle. 'You could have both been killed!'

Uncle Salman's paralysed legs move at last. He runs inside and lowers Munjed to the floor. While Aunt Nuhad joins the shouting, Munjed searches for bullets. He finds one near the front wall. It's as long as his hand and twice the width of his thumb. He examines the hole that it's made in the front wall. Another bullet has hit the rooftop air-conditioning unit. His legs tremble as he realises how close he's come to death. It will take a long time for his mother to forgive Uncle Salman.

As his father watches the family commotion, Munjed wonders whether his dad will repeat the words he loves to whisper when his mother is at her most dynamic. Sure enough, Abdul winks at his son and mutters, 'This is God's punishment to me'. Munjed giggles and runs to rescue their panicking cats.

Conjuring up money-making ventures keeps Munjed busy throughout his childhood. When Munjed is twelve, he and his cousin, Ismail, sign up for a summer school course in computer programming. Now that the Al Muderis family cannot travel overseas during summer, Munjed needs to find other ways to entertain himself.

He knows nothing about computers, but his father says technology is the way of the future. Abdul buys his son a Land Grid Array (LGA) computer which is a socket with pins that the processor is placed on. It's a very early version of the Intel Central Processing Unit (CPU). Munjed and Ismail get started on their next money-making project.

Ismail is brilliant at programming and designs a remote-controlled vehicle that is able to climb over all sorts of things. He also develops games to play on their computer screen. Their huge achievement, which they're very proud of, is creating a floating cube that turns in space. They've also replicated a tennis game with a ball bouncing from one side of the court to the other.

This is a time when not many people in Iraq know about computer programming, so the boys are soon exchanging ideas and programs with science academics. They become trailblazers, even the military are interested!

Once they tire of the computer, the teenagers carry out experiments in makeshift laboratories built in different parts of Munjed's large family home. When this becomes boring, they challenge each other on the chess board, betting their possessions on who will win each game. Before too long, Munjed has won all Ismail's prized belongings.

Munjed wants to use his innovative skills to help people and do something special with his life. He soon discovers that superheroes can come in all shapes and sizes.

The neighbourhood has a problem with hoons doing burnouts in their streets at all hours, annoying everyone. The cousins come up with a solution that is simple but effective. They buy packets of colourful balloons which they fill with water and freeze. Then they put the frozen balloons in tempting locations, mostly in gutters beside the road.

The hoons can't resist.

Drivers line up their wheels and roar towards the balloons. Instead of a satisfying pop, they hit solid objects. Some cars suffer minor damage, but no one is hurt. Most importantly, the stunned drivers go somewhere else to race, leaving Munjed's street in peace and giving him headspace to conjure his next scientific plan. It's the best one ever.

'Have you seen a Speak and Spell machine?' Munjed asks another cousin. Saheel shakes his head.

Munjed has an early model. It's basic, but the cousins have fun spelling the words that the device speaks – he especially loves the machine's robotic voice. This cousin is ten years older than Munjed and he's an electronics guru. When Saheel gets his hands on a manual that explains how to set up a radio station, the cousins don't hesitate.

The Arab Ba'ath Socialist Party that governs the country also controls all of Iraq's radio stations. Saddam Hussein doesn't want criticism or competition, especially not from two teenagers, but the cousins are curious. If they follow the instructions carefully, perhaps they really can start their own broadcasting channel. They decide to give it a go.

Using the Speak and Spell machine, Saheel and Munjed work hard to master the electronics. Their diligence is rewarded when they manage to send a signal for about a kilometre. The cousins make sure to disguise their voices.

'Good morning Baghdad, what a fine day...' Saheel alters his voice, 'We are expecting clear skies for the rest of the morning followed by another humid afternoon'.

Munjed covers his mouth to stop laughing. Then it's his turn to take the microphone.

'Here is today's puzzle. Can you solve this riddle?' Munjed clears his throat. 'What is as big as an elephant, but weighs nothing?' He pauses then answers, 'It's shadow!'

Saheel gives Munjed a thumbs up, so he asks their audience a second riddle.

'Why do fish live in salt water?'

Pause...

'Because pepper makes them sneeze.'

'And here is one more joke,' Saheel adds. 'Two men are driving home one night when one man asks the other to check if the car's indicators are working. The other man sticks his head out the window and says, "Yes, no, yes, no, yes, no, yes, no".'

The cousins laugh until their stomachs ache, but the fun ends when they see police cars patrolling their neighbourhood. Saheel flicks off the transmission.

'*Yalla.* Hurry, dismantle everything,' he yells. 'They're trying to pinpoint the radio source!'

Yalla is Arabic for *Hurry up!* or *Come on.*

They work quickly to hide the evidence. If Hussein's men find them, the consequences could be disastrous.

Once the radio is destroyed, the boys run to the kitchen, trying to look innocent as they ask for a snack. They're ecstatic that their broadcasting efforts worked, but in the process they've scared themselves witless.

3

Baghdad chessboard

'Checkmate!'

Munjed groans as his father moves a knight in check with Munjed's king. For years Munjed has tried to beat his dad at chess, but Abdul Razak Al Muderis is too good. His chess skills are legendary. Most evenings he plays from late afternoon until midnight. Sometimes his father battles ten opponents at once, and usually wins. Munjed hates losing but he doesn't want his father to *let* him win. He wants to earn his victory.

'Congratulations,' Abdul says as he sips strong Arabic coffee. 'You almost outfoxed me. You're improving.'

Munjed smiles as he packs away the chess pieces. His dad has taught him patience as well as the importance of logical thinking. One day Munjed's king will be victorious. In the meantime, he tries to be a gracious loser.

'Always strive to excel in virtue and truth,' his father whispers, as if reading Munjed's thoughts.

'Munjed,' his mother calls. 'Come and eat.'

> **Kahi** is a sweet pastry made with filo pastry that's covered with honey or sugared syrup. It's served with **Gaymer** – cream.

He sits at the table as their cook sets down a bowl of *Kahi* with *Gaymer*.

'Yum,' Munjed says between mouthfuls. It's his favourite breakfast. With the war dragging on many Iraqis are hungry, but wealthy families like the Al Muderis still eat well.

His mother hands him a glass of chilled pomegranate juice.

'Eat slowly,' she tells him, pushing a strand of hair behind her ear.

'Let's play another game of chess,' Munjed suggests, but his father shakes his head. He's reading a thick philosophy book.

'Mama?' She shakes her head as well. She's too busy to play games – their home is a meeting place for family and friends. Relations often stay for dinner and conversation long into the night. After five years of war with Iran, a new battle, the War of the Cities, has begun. SCUD missiles terrorise Baghdad at all hours of the day and night. They can reach a speed of Mach 5 (five times the speed of sound). The supersonic speed of the guided warheads fascinates Munjed, but their indiscriminate attacks mean people stay home more.

One day during one of these attacks Munjed and his cousin, Ismail, are stuck inside the house, bored. They fine-tune their latest Meccano jets and zoom between different rooms, but that's not very exciting. There are faster jets outside.

'Let's watch a movie,' Munjed suggests.

'Which one?'

'*The Terminator,* it's that new sci-fi adventure.'

The living room is cool and dark. Munjed turns on the VCR and hits play. The cousins settle back on the lounge, sipping Pepsi and sharing a big bowl of popcorn. The opening scene shows a giant machine driving over a sea of skulls in some weird, smoke-filled battle zone. Munjed is hooked.

Guns fire into the eerie darkness, then the story cuts to the rough streets of a modern city. Los Angeles, maybe? Munjed has been there and it looks familiar. The brawny Terminator appears. Ismail giggles. He isn't wearing any clothes. Munjed watches the naked cyborg uncurl like a monstrous seedling. He recognises the actor. It's Arnold Schwarzenegger, the bodybuilder.

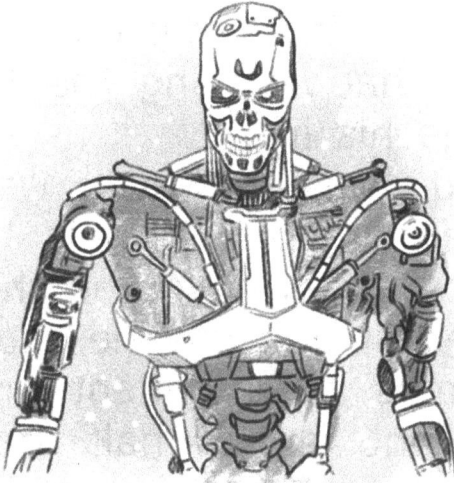

As the Terminator strides away to steal clothes, he comes across a group of punks.

'*Nice night for a walk,*' one punk says.

'*Nice night for a walk,*' the Terminator mimics.

'*Wash day tomorrow!*' says punk guy. '*Nothing clean, right?*

'*Nothing clean. Right.*'

Munjed is fascinated. The Terminator is part man, part machine. Underneath its living tissue of skin, blood and hair, is a hyper-alloy combat chassis, microprocessor controlled, fully armoured cyborg. He moves closer to the television as the cyborg carefully repairs the hardware inside his arm. This is the best movie he's ever seen. He doesn't know then that watching *The Terminator* will change his life.

Munjed has always wanted to become a surgeon. As this half man, half robot causes havoc on the screen, he wonders if one day he could attach robotic limbs to a patient and create someone who is also half robotic. The Baghdad streets are full of amputees and war-disabled beggars. Helping them walk again would be amazing.

His mother brings the cousins a plate of figs and slices of melon. She frowns at The Terminator's rotting skin as a cleaner asks Schwarzenegger, *'Hey, buddy. You got a dead cat in there?'*

'What are you boys watching?'

'*The Terminator.* He's a cyborg,' Munjed points to the screen. 'Imagine if one day I learnt to make a human-machine like that.'

'If anyone can, you will.' She ruffles his hair. 'Remember when you were four?'

His cousin grins as Munjed groans. This is his mother's favourite story.

'Not many four-year-olds could use a pair of pliers the way you did to take off your jangling foot bangle,' Kamila smiles proudly. 'And then, what a dexterous little fellow, you attached it to the cat.'

Munjed remembers the tinkle of bells and outraged look on the cat's face.

'You'll be a great surgeon one day,' she continues, as Arnold Schwarzenegger's skin peels back to reveal his powerful endoskeleton. 'I know it.'

The rampaging cyborg explodes onto the screen. Forget chess and Meccano, Munjed thinks. Attaching robotic limbs to humans is what he wants to do. A pivotal scene from the movie replays in his mind, over and over. It's a conversation between the heroine, Sarah, and the soldier who has travelled back in time to save her:

Sarah: *'They cannot make things like that'.*

Kyle: *'Not yet. Not for about 40 years'.*

Sarah: *'Are you saying it's from the future?'* Kyle: *'One possible future. From your point of view ... I don't know tech stuff'.*

Sarah: *'Then you're from the future, too. Is that right?'*

Kyle: *'Right'.*

***

After Ismail leaves, Munjed wanders into the garden. He lies underneath a palm tree and stares up at the frond-patterned sky, wondering about his future. Everything depends on the war and when it will end, but if he *does* become a surgeon, maybe he really could perform robotics. The Kyle character said 40 years. Munjed would be over 50 by then. Would that be too old to perform complicated operations? Perhaps the technology could be developed sooner.

A jet screams over the city.

'Munjed,' his mother calls, 'come inside.' He sighs.

'I'll be back!' Munjed shouts to the sky as he races inside.

Wondering where the SCUD missiles will strike puts everyone on edge. Munjed feels as if his life is a spinning wheel of fortune where he has gone from the top to the bottom. His family's privileged cosmopolitan neighbourhood is now a war zone. The Iraqi economy is crippled by the war. Professional families no longer have an income. His neighbours have moved to safer areas.

Munjed realises that things will never be the same again, but his father has impressed upon him the importance of seeing the world as a glass that is half full, instead of half empty.

During the darkest days, he tells himself: 'We all have a mission in life, and mine is to be a surgeon'.

When the wheel of fortune rotates upwards, Munjed will be ready to grab opportunities with both hands. In the meantime, he practises his chess moves – there are different paths to success. He experiments with pawn openings, tricky knight moves and strategic castling, determined to outfox his father one day. He also studies hard at school so that his grades are good enough for him to get into medicine at university.

Luckily, there are many doctors in his family to give him help and inspiration. His cousin, Fadhel, is a military surgeon and his father's cousin, Allah Bashir, is a skillful plastic surgeon. When he tells them he's fascinated with reconstructive surgery, his uncle suggests dentistry.

'There's a lot of reconstructing with that.'

'No, I want to replace limbs and help amputees.'

Uncle Bashir takes young Munjed to his surgery and lets him watch a hand re-implantation operation where he removes the patient's damaged tissue, then shortens the bone ends, ready to re-join the hand and fingers with pins, plates and screws. His uncle's hand is steady as he attaches the hardware that will hold everything in place while the body's own tissue regrows. After repairing his patient's muscles, tendons, nerves and veins, Uncle Bashir steps aside to allow an assistant to close the incision. The operation requires great skill. Munjed is incredibly impressed.

'Will the patient's hand work normally?' he asks.

'That depends,' Uncle Bashir replies. 'Many factors add to an operation's success. I'll be hoping for at least 60 to 80 per cent hand use.'

His uncle smiles at Munjed.

'Did you enjoy the operation?'

'It was amazing.'

Uncle Bashir nods.

'You're like me,' he chuckles. 'Now off you go, I need to read the notes for my next patient's surgery. It's a facial reconstruction.'

'Can I watch?'

'If you want to...'

Munjed sits quietly transfixed as Uncle Bashir makes his first incision. The operation is gruesome, bloody and compelling. Munjed loves it. As he watches his uncle's hands rebuild a face, Munjed knows more than ever, that he *must* become a surgeon. He'll do whatever it takes to achieve his goal.

4

1989/91: Bullies, bombs and books

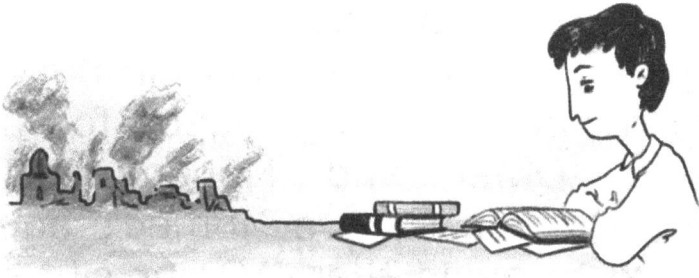

Avoiding bullies at high school is like tiptoeing over a minefield. In the late 1980s Baghdad College has hundreds of students and Munjed's private school is now open to all. Many of the new students act like hoodlums.

Saddam Hussein's sons, Udai and Qusay, attend Baghdad College and they're the worst thugs. Udai is older than Munjed. He's smart in a cunning way. Qusay is not smart like his brother but he's just as much a bully, strutting around the school with his bodyguards, ignoring all of the rules. Vehicles are forbidden in the school grounds, but Qusay roars about on his quad bike. The Hussein brothers think it's hilarious and no one dares to stop them – not even the teachers. Later, these teenage thugs will graduate to commit dreadful crimes on an epic scale.

Qusay is six years older than Munjed. He's left school by the time Munjed arrives but the Hussein brothers leave behind a strong legacy for their cousins, Omar and Mohammed, to follow. The cousins are Munjed's age so it's hard to avoid them. Omar sits next to Munjed in class and he does whatever he likes. Munjed avoids talking to him, but it's difficult to ignore him completely.

One time when Munjed and his friend Manaf are walking across the quadrangle, Omar starts throwing stones at them, yelling, 'Hey, are you Shi'ite or Sunni?'

'I don't know what you mean,' Munjed replies, carefully. He has no strong religious beliefs.

Omar laughs at him. 'You're an idiot,' he mocks, walking away.

It feels like a lucky escape.

Each year there are school elections and Omar bullies his way onto the Student Council, following in the footsteps of Mudar, his older brother. A few years earlier Mudar lost his own school election, so his bodyguards beat up the winner. They broke the teenager's back and left him for dead in a river. The young man survived but was paralysed for life. Munjed worries that if he offends Omar, he might suffer a similar fate.

Unsurprisingly, science is Munjed's favourite subject at school, but he also plays soccer, as a striker. Munjed scores plenty of goals, but Omar is in the other school team and Omar's team *always* has to win. Although it runs against his competitive nature,

Munjed is careful to miss a few shots whenever he plays against Omar's team. Munjed and his friends love television, but there are only two channels. They're both run by Saddam Hussein's regime and the programs are mostly about how great Saddam is. There's nothing of interest for teenage Munjed. In the evening, when transmission ends, the screen becomes electronic snow accompanied by a weird buzz.

'It's Saddam snoring,' people joke behind closed doors where only their family can hear.

One of Munjed's favourite movies at this time is *E.T.* He first saw the film when he was ten, but the memory stays with him during high school and sparks an audacious communications project. Munjed is fed up with the state-run media which broadcast endless propaganda about the regime. He's read about satellite communication, so he decides to try something new even though it's incredibly risky.

Without telling his parents, he buys a satellite dish that has been smuggled into Iraq so he and his cousin, Saheel, can set up their own entertainment system. They know that the punishment for even having a dish is severe and can include execution. But they do it anyway.

The dish needs to be hidden from the 'eyes in the sky' – the helicopters that fly over Baghdad every day searching for illegal communication devices. Munjed has the bright idea of building a chicken coop on the roof, which he covers with feathers. It perfectly camouflages their secret satellite dish.

When everything is up and running, he invites a few trustworthy friends to his house to watch programs from Israel, Turkey, Italy, Germany and beyond. Best of all, they're able to tune into MTV. They watch video countdown, live concerts with their favourite rock stars and follow beach culture shows like *Spring Break.* It opens up the world to them, but they're careful to only watch TV late at night after the helicopter 'eyes' have stopped flying.

***

Although going to university during wartime will be challenging, Munjed is determined to enrol in medical school, preferably in the USA where he knows there are world-leading teachers and hospitals. By the beginning of August 1990, his dream is about to come true – he's been accepted into New York University and everything is in place. He's enrolled, paid tuition fees, booked his flight and is ready to go.

Kuwait is a country next to The Gulf and flanked by Iran, Iraq and Saudi Arabia. It is tiny but its strategic location and massive oil reserves mean it is of great interest politically. It is also one of the richest countries per capita.

Then, on 2 August, 1990, Saddam Hussein's army invades Kuwait – a country next to Iraq which is a US ally. This means Munjed can no longer study in America.

It seems that the wheel of fortune has turned again, this time, downwards.

Despite Munjed's usual optimism, for a while his glass seems half-empty. But he knows there's no point in feeling sorry for himself. The deadline for applications to study medicine at nearby Baghdad University has closed. Where else can he go?

He decides to make a last-minute application to Basra University.

It has a good medical school, but the city is in southern Iraq, close to the Iraqi-Kuwaiti border. And it's a five-hour drive from Baghdad along a road which will soon be known as 'The Highway of Death'.

Munjed's application is accepted. He moves south to begin his studies.

Once a beautiful, cosmopolitan city, Basra's infrastructure has been devastated from years of war with Iran. When Munjed arrives in September 1990, there are daily blackouts. The hospitals are desperately short of supplies, the water quality is poor and the roads have been heavily bombed. There are holes large enough for a car to fall into!

He moves in with a cousin and registers at the university. Students come from across Iraq. Those from Baghdad, like Munjed, wear colourful

Western outfits while the locals wear traditional clothes in softer colours. At first the Sunnis, Shi'ites and Christians only socialise in their own groups, but gradually the students mix more freely.

Saddam's invasion of Kuwait is complete in just a few days – the Kuwaiti soldiers are no match for the world's fourth largest army. The aftermath of the conflict is more complicated. Under pressure from the US, the United Nations sets a deadline for Iraq to withdraw from Kuwait by January 1991.

***

As that withdrawal date approaches, Munjed is studying for his mid-year exams. He senses an uneasy feeling across the city even though he spends almost every moment studying.

Then, after his Biology exam, in the early hours of January 17, Munjed is woken by the sound of shrieking warplanes and bomb blasts. Saddam Hussein has **not** agreed to the deadline. US bombers are leading a massive aerial attack on Iraq, and Basra, a city near the Kuwaiti border, is a major target.

At first light, Munjed drives to the hospital, knowing there will be heavy casualties. The chaotic scenes that greet him are worse than any nightmare.

'Quick, stem that patient's bleeding!'

'Doctor, please help me.'

'Get a drip into that patient...'

Everywhere he looks there are horrifically injured people – they cram the Emergency Department, hospital wards and corridors. Along with other medical students Munjed spends all day helping to splint broken bones, remove shrapnel and clean wounds. His dream of practising medicine didn't include this.

As the bombing continues, he worries about his parents, knowing that Baghdad will also be under siege. His parents recently moved to the outskirts of the capital but there's no way to contact them. The bombing has cut all phone lines. Munjed is desperate to be with his family right now, but how can he get there? The refineries and petrol stations have been hit so fuel is almost impossible to come by.

In the evening Munjed drives to a friend's home, hoping to find a way. Luckily an engineer who is also keen to return to Baghdad is at the house.

'Let's pool resources,' he suggests.

Munjed has a car with badly worn tyres but he does not have enough petrol to make the 550-kilometre trip.

'Don't worry about that,' the engineer says. 'I know people in Samawah. If we go together, I'll arrange for us to fill up there.'

There are two roads to Baghdad. Samawah is about halfway to the city on an old desert road. Even in peacetime it's a dangerous route. And the road passes the biggest military airbase in Iraq – a clear target for American bombers. To get to the capital, Munjed and his companion will need to drive through a harsh desert region then somehow get fuel and drive past an airbase that will be under attack from the world's most powerful military force. And all of this on roads that may be impassable!

This is crazy, Munjed thinks. But what if the war continues for weeks or months? Things could get much worse and being with family is his priority. He decides to take a chance.

They set off early the next morning, driving out of bomb-blasted Basra towards the Euphrates River. Although bridges are down, Iraqi military engineering teams are busy rebuilding them. Driving over the makeshift bridges as US aircraft rumble overhead is terrifying, but their luck holds; the bombers fly on to other targets.

As they approach the Imam Ali Airbase, Munjed drives as fast as he can. Dust and smoke cover the road. He has to swerve to avoid bomb craters. It's hard not to panic. His companion helps by giving a steady stream of advice in a calm voice.

'Watch out for that crater! Don't look at anything except the road...'

Explosions thunder around them, shaking the car. The thudding is just metres away. Sirens wail. Munjed is sure he's going to die. He grips the steering wheel and drives doggedly on, foot pressing the accelerator to the floor.

'Don't look at anything except the road,' the engineer repeats.

They are the only car on a six-lane highway. It feels bizarre and frightening. Burnt out military vehicles litter the sides of the road and Munjed sees bombed power plants. Replacing them will take months or even years. Somehow, they get through. It seems miraculous. The airbase is behind them, but the car is very low on fuel. The warning light flashes. They must reach Samawah soon...

At last they reach the town, just as they think there can't be a drop of petrol left in the tank. The engineer manages to get some fuel from someone he knows, but it's too dangerous to rest.

'Keep driving,' he mutters, urgently.

Munjed needs no convincing, flooring the accelerator and driving non-stop until dusk, when they finally reach his parents' safe house in Suhwayrah, not far from Baghdad.

***

As he walks into the house alive and unharmed, Munjed's mother collapses in relief. His parents have moved to Suwayrah because they thought it would be safe; but Suwayrah, too, is under constant attack. Unbeknown to the Al Muderis family, this normally sleepy country town now has a division of the Republican Guard based there. A rocket launching area is also nearby. So is a helicopter base.

The **Republican Guard** *are elite troops who* typically serve to protect the head of state, in this case Saddam Hussein. They are generally better trained, disciplined, equipped, and paid more than ordinary Iraqi soldiers.

The town is an obvious target for coalition bombers, and the attacks are relentless.

Each night Munjed is kept awake by the noise of nearby explosions. Some evenings he sits on the top floor of the Al Muderis's safe house watching American bombing raids. Will I ever be able to complete medical school, he wonders as shrapnel smashes into buildings. Fortunately, the local library is not hit so Munjed goes there every day trying to continue his studies. One day he sees something astonishing and heartwarming.

As planes fly overhead on yet another bombing mission, a truck from a local dairy pulls up near the market. The driver throws open the doors.

'Free ice cream,' he calls. 'Enjoy a treat before it melts.'

'Why is it free?' Munjed asks.

'We have no electricity,' the man replies. 'I'd rather give the ice cream away than see it wasted.'

As children jiggle with happiness Munjed learns that free milk will also be available.

'Our cows need to be milked whether the power is on or off. Bring a container. We'll be here at 7.30 in the morning.'

Munjed is deeply touched by this act of kindness in the midst of such horror. He vows then and there to be like the dairy farmer: to always give back more than he takes from society.

Suwayrah remains Munjed's home for the rest of the war. Occasionally he risks taking a trip to Baghdad where he sees the heartbreaking aftermath of the bombing. Beautiful old bridges and buildings are destroyed. He can hardly believe what he is seeing. It's the most awful sight, the city he grew up in, ruined, and for what, he wonders.

Like most Iraqis, Munjed's family are deeply affected by the war. Nine members of his aunt's family, including six children, are killed along with 400 other innocent people in just one horrific incident known as the Al Ameriya Bunker Disaster. During another air raid, his cousin Saheel is buried alive.

After hours trapped under rubble, Saheel's rescuers dig him out. Although his body heals, from then on, he suffers ongoing Post Traumatic Stress Disorder (PTSD) and is never the same. Whenever Munjed sees his broken cousin, he remembers the childhood days of watching videos and eating popcorn together. They seem so far away and so innocent.

During the darkest moments, Munjed whispers the words of Khalil Gibran, the famous Lebanese-American poet and one of his father's favourites: 'Out of suffering have emerged the strongest souls; the most massive characters are seared with scars'.

Munjed draws courage from this wisdom, but some days it's hard to be resilient, to be brave, especially when he sees how the war has aged his parents.

On 3 March 1991, there is a ceasefire and Saddam Hussein orders Iraqi military withdrawal from Kuwait. The Al Muderis family returns home. But Baghdad is no longer a city of plenty. There is no electricity and no petrol for cars. People look frightened. Many have lost family members and everyone has seen the horrors of war.

Munjed resumes his medical studies and works hard although with so much sadness and chaos, staying focused is an ongoing challenge. There are so many more amputees in the streets now. This war has made him even more determined to become a surgeon and help them.

**

The war has also taken a heavy toll on the health of Abdul Razak Al Muderis. This proud man is now confined to a wheelchair. When he dies a few years later at the age of 91, it leaves a huge hole in Munjed's life. He loses his father and his mentor.

According to tradition, the deceased's body should be buried before sunset. Abdul is laid to rest in Islamic style, wrapped in a white shroud with his head resting on a stone pillow, facing Mecca, the birthplace of Muhammad.

Although Munjed and his family are not religious, they follow the traditional funeral rituals that extend over three days. Munjed sits by the gate, hiding his tears as he welcomes mourners, wishing he could be alone with his grief.

As he waits for the rituals to end, Munjed remembers his father's words, 'You are a cog on the wheel of fortune. There will be outside influences, but the one who steers is you.'

Munjed takes his father's advice and in 1996 he qualifies as a medical practitioner. After completing his internship, he's accepted into the surgical training program.

5

1999: First, do no harm

By the late 1990s, Iraq has become a terrible place to live. Economic hardship and religious intolerance affect everyone. In 1999, all Iraqi men who were born in 1972 are called up for military service. Those who refuse are labelled deserters. Munjed is working as an intern at the Saddam Hussein Medical Centre in Baghdad at this stage and he is lucky because as a doctor he is exempt from the call-up order.

Hospital conditions are very difficult for all the staff because there is an extreme lack of medical supplies. Everyone has to do the best they can with what is available. Disposable suture material is sterilised and re-used, when it should be thrown away. Surgical gloves that are normally only used once are re-used. This means patients risk infections that could make them dangerously sick. Plates, nails and screws used to hold broken bones in one patient are sterilised and re-used in another patient. And there are no prostheses available for people who have lost an arm or a leg.

Many of Munjed patients come in with gunshot wounds, as firing guns into the air is something Iraqis love to do when celebrating, whether it's at weddings or after a national sporting success. Once, when the Iraqi soccer team won in a World Cup match, over 1,000 people with bullet wounds were admitted to hospitals across the country.

'How can people be so stupid?' he mutters, amazed that they don't stop to think that if you fire a bullet into the air, it has to come down somewhere.

One autumn morning Munjed arrives at the hospital early and meets with the senior surgeons and registrars to discuss new admissions. Then he visits his patients on the wards. They're all recovering well so he checks the surgery list. The first operation is difficult. There are techniques he's eager to learn so he hopes he'll be allowed to assist. The patient's injury is caused by gunfire and a bullet has landed in a young girl's chest.

Munjed joins the other doctors in the operating theatre.

'The wound is particularly complicated,' the senior surgeon says.

As they discuss how best to reach the bullet, their meeting is suddenly interrupted. A squad of Republican Guards storms in, led by a powerfully built officer. He strides towards the doctors.

'Cancel all surgeries,' he shouts.

'I beg your pardon—'

Three busloads of shivering men have arrived outside. Munjed watches the wretched prisoners shuffle into the admissions area. Some are bloody and beaten. Other men are in pyjamas. They look as if they've been dragged from their beds. Three burly officers march down the corridor barking orders.

'Prepare to operate on these deserters!' the officer yells as soldiers herd the men. 'You will cut off part of each traitor's ear.'

Munjed shudders. He can't believe how calm the prisoners are.

'Lie down on trolleys,' the senior officer tells them.

Perhaps the prisoners believe losing an ear is better than torture. Or amputation without anaesthetic. Or death.

Munjed remembers the day Saddam's henchmen arrested his neighbour for failing to join up to military service. The young man was hauled out of the house in just his underwear.

'Don't take my boy,' his mother screamed.

Behind the woman a loudspeaker urged people to come and watch the man's execution. After a firing squad shot the neighbour, his family were forced to disown their son and pay for the bullets that killed their boy.

Munjed pinches his nose to steady his breathing. These soldiers look just as ruthless as those henchmen. They're dressed in camouflage uniforms with heavy combat boots that echo as they stomp along the hospital corridor.

'Begin the surgery now!'

Munjed stares at the soldier's rifles and wonders, what can he do? Then he hears a voice. It's the Head of Surgery.

'As doctors we have sworn to follow the Hippocratic Oath,' the surgeon says. 'That oath states, *First, do no harm.*' The Head of Surgery takes a deep breath. 'Disfiguring these men would be acting against that vow.'

The army officer scowls.

'These orders come from Saddam Hussein.'

'I'm sorry,' the doctor repeats bravely. 'We must first, do no harm.'

'Take this man outside,' the officer orders.

Soldiers drag the surgeon into the car park. Munjed hears a gunshot.

'Now that we have your attention,' the soldier warns, 'if anyone else shares this man's view, step forward. Otherwise, proceed with your orders.'

Munjed scans the terrified faces around him. His colleagues are immobilised with fear. Munjed can't maim a patient. That would go against everything he believes in. But if he refuses, he too will be shot.

He stares at the ears of the prisoners. His mind is going crazy, remembering facts about ear anatomy that he's learnt during medical training.

Why is he remembering this *now?*

- **Ears** are home to our sense of balance.
- The hardest bone in the body protects the inner ear.
- The smallest bone, a weirdly shaped stirrup, is nestled deep in the inner ear.
- Ear wax may be gross but it's important for protecting the ear canal.

Munjed looks around the room. Focus, he tells himself. *Focus.*

His father has impressed on him that if you think your actions will harm someone, then it is better not to act, no matter what any religious book or doctrine tells you. But right now there is no way to get past the soldiers.

'Now!' the officer yells.

Munjed knows he cannot obey the officer's barbaric orders. He faces the greatest dilemma of his life. Holding firm to his beliefs means that he will probably die today, but in the meantime, he makes a quick decision. He will *try* to survive.

While everyone is distracted, he steps slowly backwards then slips away to the women's bathroom and rushes into a cubicle. Locking the door, he sits down on the toilet. His hands are shaking as memories of other bullies crowd his mind. He remembers Saddam's nephews strutting around the schoolyard and how powerless the other students were in the face of their random cruelty. The best anyone could do was keep out of the thugs' way.

The injustice of that time and today's dilemma burn inside him. If Munjed wants to be an instrument for change, he has to stay alive. That means he must escape. Otherwise he will be executed.

Munjed remembers his father's favourite Islamic quote: *None of you truly believes until he wishes for his brother what he wishes for himself.* The words are similar to the Christian Golden Rule: *Do unto others as you would have them do unto you.* These are sentiments the Al Muderis family has always lived by.

What would his father, Abdul Razak Al Muderis do, Munjed wonders? At this moment, he desperately misses his father's wise counsel, but the answer is clear. Abdul always encouraged Munjed to question rules, to chart his own course in life and refuse orders that violate the principles he was brought up with. He stays on the toilet.

Hours pass. The tension is unbearable. Munjed stares at the floor tiles, trying desperately to think of ways to escape. He's incredibly thirsty – he knows that's what happens when adrenaline flushes through your body. But he can't move, not yet.

Each time nurses come in, he holds his breath. They use another toilet. Munjed shivers when several women come in together to clean their hands. If he is discovered, the soldiers will haul him away to be shot. Or tortured and then shot.

Luckily, no one hears his frightened breathing or notices that one toilet, the second last of five cubicles, has been occupied all afternoon.

After five terrifying hours, a group of nurses come in to wash up after the horrors they've been forced to perform.

They leave and Munjed waits another fifteen minutes. He needs to be absolutely sure that the mutilation surgery is over. Each minute feels like an hour.

He is now a traitor and in Iraq, traitors are shot.

The minutes pass.

At last, he peeks out of the women's bathroom. The corridor is quiet. He crosses the hall, runs into the men's changing rooms, sheds his surgical gown and pulls on street clothes from his locker.

Sweat trickles down his back. Where can he go?

His legs want to run, but he forces them to stroll across the crowded hospital foyer, keeping his head down, avoiding eye contact. It seems an age till he pushes the door and exits into soft sunlight.

He heads for the nearest bus station. It's too dangerous to take his own car and he can't return home. The soldiers might already be there. Endangering his mum is not an option.

The wheel of fortune has turned again. Munjed can't stay in Baghdad anymore so he must risk his life and try to escape.

But where to? The choices are limited. Munjed knows people in Suwayrah, Basra and Ramadi. He weighs up the pros and cons of each.

- Suwayrah is uncomfortably close to Baghdad. Being further away would be safer.
- Basra is 500 kilometres away, near the Kuwaiti border, but Iraqis are no longer welcome in that country.

- Ramadi is a traditional town where Munjed studied for a year. People there tend to keep to themselves. That might work in his favour.

He decides that Ramadi is the safest option. He keeps walking, trying to appear casual. Halfway to the bus station, he hails a taxi and gives the driver the address of a friend's house, a friend he hopes he can trust. Ali is a doctor, too, and now Munjed's life will be in his hands.

The taxi ride takes 25 minutes. When Munjed knocks on Ali's door, his surprised friend invites him in.

'Something horrible has happened,' Munjed whispers. 'I need to get out of Baghdad. Can you help me?'

6

1999: Fleeing for his life...

Ali grabs a jacket and drives Munjed to a nearby café. He listens to his friend's story and agrees without hesitation to drive him to safety.

'*Yalla,*' Ali says, 'let's go'.

They set off for Ramadi. Munjed feels numb. In one day his entire life has changed. He is 27 and is taking the first step of a journey away from his family and his dreams of becoming a surgeon.

It's a 90-minute trip and they must pass through two checkpoints staffed by military police. The officers are looking for army deserters. As doctors, Munjed and Ali are exempt from serving but staying calm is difficult. Munjed squeezes his earlobes and feels his blood pressure rise as the police scrutinise his papers.

They pass the first checkpoint. Munjed breathes out in relief. Their papers are checked again at the second barrier. The doctors keep their faces calm and politely answer each question. They are allowed through.

Once the checkpoint is a few kilometres behind them, Ali drives as fast as he can without breaking the speed limit. They arrive at Ramadi just before dusk. Munjed knocks at the door of another friend, Nissan, the next person to whom he will trust his life. As Nissan opens the door, Ali turns to drive back to Baghdad.

'Good luck.'

'Thank you,' Munjed whispers to his friend, clasping his hand.

Ali nods. 'I'll try to contact your mother and let her know you're safe...'

Nissan invites Munjed to stay and shows him to a guestroom that's well away from other family members.

When he hears Munjed's story, Nissan says, 'You cannot return'.

'I know,' Munjed replies, unhappily.

They drink tea and devise a plan to smuggle him out of the country. He has no other choice.

While Munjed stays in the house, Nissan drives to Baghdad and checks on Munjed's mother. Nissan is taking a huge risk just to go there. If he is followed, the outcome will be disastrous for them both. Sure enough, the Ba'ath Party officials have already been to the house to question her.

The **Arab Socialist Ba'ath Party** is a political party who believe in the unification of the Arab world into a single state and freedom from non-Arab control and interference. In Munjed's time, it had branches in many Middle Eastern countries and was the ruling party in Iraq from 1968-2003, under the leadership of Saddam Hussein.

'I haven't seen Munjed since the morning when he went to work,' she was able to tell them truthfully.

They look around nervously, wondering if they're being watched. Kamila gives Nissan an envelope holding US $ 12,000 in cash.

'Munjed will need money to help him escape,' she says.

Nissan returns to Ramadi and the next evening he and Munjed meet two scary looking men in a café. They're tall, powerfully built and have enormous moustaches. The men are senior passport officers. They demand a $ 5000 deposit for a fake passport, and another $ 5000 when they deliver it.

Luckily, Munjed's cousin, Bassam, works at the Passport Office so he offers to liaise with the corrupt, moustachioed officers, organising papers and getting photos from Kamila.

He also manages to get together $ 20,000 so Munjed will have cash to take with him after paying off the passport officers.

While Munjed waits for the passport to be made, he sneaks back to visit his mother, hoping no one will recognise him. If they do, he will be arrested and killed. Kamila is relieved to see her son but weeps as she holds him. Then she hands him the cash.

'Now quick, hide it. Who knows what challenges lie ahead. This money will smooth the way. I hope it's enough to keep you safe.'

Munjed hugs his mother and, with deep sadness in his heart, he returns to Ramadi where he takes delivery of his new passport. It looks just like his real one except that instead of Munjed Al Muderis, junior surgeon, he has become Munjed Al Muderis, handyman. Munjed flexes his smooth, non-calloused hands. He will need to keep them hidden.

There is still one huge obstacle. Doctors are forbidden from leaving the country and despite the new passport, Munjed's name will be on a computer list of people who must stay in Iraq. Bassam's friends inside the Passport Office are unable to permanently wipe Munjed's name from that list, but they can block the data at one border crossing for a few hours.

It's a huge risk, but again, Munjed has no choice. If he were a chessboard king he'd be in check, but hopefully he is not yet in checkmate.

'Handyman' Munjed is given instructions to travel to Baghdad then board a bus bound for Jordan. He must arrive at the Trebil border crossing by mid-afternoon, when the data will be blocked.

So many things can go wrong. Even the first step, returning to Baghdad, is terrifying for Munjed. What if he is recognised or the bus to Jordan is delayed and he misses the block-out time?

When he reaches the Baghdad bus station, Munjed's mother and cousin, Bassam, are waiting to farewell him. Their presence gives him courage, especially as armed guards swarm around the depot. His mother is in tears, but Munjed forces himself to hold back his emotions – if the guards suspect anything is out of the ordinary, he will be questioned.

Waiting for the bus to take him to Jordan is nerve-wracking. His mother's money is taped tightly around his stomach. It feels bulky but strangely comforting. When the bus finally arrives, Munjed hugs his mother one last time.

'Goodbye, my son,' she whispers. As he takes his seat, he wonders whether he'll ever see her again.

***

The journey to Jordan begins smoothly. Staring across the five-lane highway as they drive west, he can't help remembering the frightening trip from Amman when he was eight. This modern bus is totally different from that old rust bucket, but his fear is just as sharp, or even more so without the calming presence of his father. Even though it's been four years since Abdul Razak passed away, Munjed misses his dad every day. Grief wraps around him like a cloak, the bleak desert landscape matching his mood.

Pulling your ear lobes stimulates the **vagus nerve,** which runs from the brain through the face and chest down to the abdomen. It sends a message to your heart to slow down. Try it yourself!

To lessen his anxiety, Munjed uses his old trick of pulling his ear lobes. Then he alternates his nostril breathing. He *must* look calm, not nervous, when he arrives at the border crossing. His life depends on it.

Munjed keeps checking his watch during the journey. What if the Passport Officers have not been able to remove his name from the list? And what if the bus doesn't arrive during the time when the data is blocked? His hands start to shake so he pulls his ear lobes again.

Eventually they reach the dusty border post of Trebil. The bus is on time!

Munjed follows other passengers into the immigration building and takes his place in the queue. While the officials are not looking at him, he carefully rearranges his shirt over the hidden money. It feels bulky. What if they notice?

All is going well ... until he reaches the immigration counter.

There are three passport control officers. With sudden horror, Munjed realises that he recognises the man sitting behind one desk, and worse, he knows that man could recognise him!

Six weeks earlier, Munjed stitched the badly gashed wrist of an officer who'd been involved in a bar-room brawl. This is the same man. Sweat breaks out along Munjed's spine. There are two chances in three that Munjed will stand before one of the other officers, but what if he gets the third? His life is at another crossroad. Should he keep going and risk his life? Or turn back now?

But there is no real choice – he has to go on. He keeps his head down. The man was drunk when Munjed stemmed the bleeding and stitched his hand. Maybe he won't recognise the doctor who patched him up.

'Please, please, please...' he whispers, as the line moves forward.

'Next,' the officer next to his former patient calls.

That's it, Munjed thinks. *I'm done for if my former patient sees me.*

He steps forward. The officer looks up briefly and leafs through Munjed's passport.

'What is your job?' he asks.

'I'm a handyman.'

'And what are you doing in Jordan?'

'Getting some parts for an air conditioner.'

'How long will you stay?'

'About a month.'

'How much money do you have with you?'

'One thousand US dollars.'

The man is surprised. 'That's a lot for a month.'

'Maybe I'll stay longer...'

The man looks bored. He nods and stamps Munjed's passport.

'Have a nice trip.'

Munjed struggles to keep his face calm. The ordeal is not over yet. His luggage also needs to be checked. That's okay, but then there is a body search. Luckily, the Iraqi officials don't notice the money strapped to Munjed's stomach. They wave him through.

He's almost safe...

There's another wait as the bus is carefully examined. At any moment, Munjed imagines someone suddenly recognising him and shouting, **STOP!**

Finally, the passengers climb back on board, to drive for another three hours across No Man's Land. The Jordanian road soon becomes a rough, potholed track, but none of that matters to Munjed.

He has escaped Iraq.

7

Nowhere to go

They reach Amman as the sun rises which seems like a good omen. Munjed is welcomed into an uncle's home to enjoy a well-earned rest, but he has no idea what to do after that.

'There's no work at the hospitals,' his uncle tells him when he wakes up. 'And the city is filled with Iraqi secret service agents.'

It's too dangerous to stay, but since the war, few countries will accept travellers on an Iraqi passport. Malaysia is an exception. Perhaps he can find medical work there. Munjed's dream of becoming a surgeon seems unattainable now, but if he enrols in a Malaysian Master of Surgery degree, perhaps he could work as an unpaid intern in Kuala Lumpur, the capital of Malaysia. At least he would be practising medicine.

After a week of feeling more and more uneasy in Amman, Munjed thanks his uncle and books a flight to Kuala Lumpur. At the airport he paces around the departure hall, hoping his false passport won't be scrutinised too closely. As he waits in another immigration line he feels his anxiety rising. The official looks him up and down, hesitates for a moment, then stamps the passport. Munjed takes a deep breath. The forgers have done a good job.

The flight to Malaysia goes via Abu Dhabi. In the United Arab Emirates transit lounge, immigration officers ask for the passports of all Iraqi travellers.

'What's going on?' two men protest in Arabic, but the only way to communicate with the officials is in English.

Munjed offers to interpret. The travellers are wary.

'We are tourists,' they tell him, but their calloused hands and second-hand clothes tell another story.

Munjed translates essential travel documents for the two men, and then again when they land in Malaysia, not knowing that the wheel of fortune has caught him in its cogs and that this chance meeting will determine his future.

As soon as his new companions, Hussein and Ali, clear immigration in the Kuala Lumpur airport, they look for a public telephone. The phone operating instructions are in English so once again they need Munjed's help. He dials, hands the phone to Hussein and is shocked to discover that Ali and Hussein are making contact with people smugglers.

The smuggler tells the men to take a taxi to the Chow Kit area. Munjed gives the driver instructions while Ali and Hussein sit in the back. As they drive he wonders how on earth his fellow escapees would have managed all this on their own.

Chow Kit is a bustling shopping district. They wait where they've been told to. A tall Western-looking man approaches and takes them to a dingy backpacker hostel.

'You'll need to give me your passports and $ 450 each.'

Munjed is reluctant to hand over his most-treasured possession – his passport – to a people-smuggler. This was never part of his plans.

'How do I know I can trust you?' he asks.

'How dare you question my credibility! I am a respectable smuggler and I have a reputation to protect, and you have no choice. Take it or leave it.'

The other men hand over their passports. Munjed hesitates. He has no idea how the process works.

'My job is to get you to Indonesia,' the smuggler says, shrugging. 'From there onward, I don't know.'

Munjed considers his options. Malaysia is not a signatory to the 1951 Refugee Convention or the 1967 Protocol. If he tries to claim asylum, the Malaysian authorities might send him back to Iraq. That would probably mean death.

'I don't have all day...'

The **1951 Refugee Convention** and its **1967 Protocol** define what a refugee is, their rights, and a country's legal obligations to protect them. It states that a refugee should not be returned to a country where they face serious threats to their life or freedom.

Taking a deep breath, he hands over the cash and his passport, as well as extra money for a plane ticket to Jakarta, the capital of Indonesia.

Afterwards, the three men leave the hotel to share a meal. Munjed is so anxious he can barely swallow. Has he made a terrible mistake?

A few hours later their passports are returned along with tickets for a Garuda flight. Everything is happening so quickly.

'When you get to Jakarta, call this number,' the smuggler tells them, handing Munjed a slip of paper. Then he explains what they'll need to do at Indonesian Immigration.

'There will be several desks. Do not go to the woman and do not go to the Chief Immigration Officer. Look for the guy who has one star on his uniform. When you give him your passport, make sure there is $ 100 inside and keep the passport closed.'

'Hang on, are you expecting me to bribe a customs officer in a major international airport?'

'Yes,' he replies calmly. 'Do you have a problem with that?'

'No, I just thought I would check.' Munjed knows he simply has no choice at this point.

There is a day to fill before the flight to Indonesia. Munjed walks around the bustling city then visits a friend's sister and brother-in-law. They are working in Kuala Lumpur and are horrified to hear about the people smuggling plan.

'We can help you find work here,' they offer.

Munjed thanks them but realises that even if he pays to study in Malaysia, he's unlikely to be able to practise medicine unless it's voluntary work. Despite everything, Munjed's dream of becoming a surgeon is still not *totally* extinguished.

The flight to Jakarta is uneventful and on arrival, they follow the people smuggler's instructions. The immigration room is exactly as he has described. Ali, Hussein and Munjed hand their passports to the man with one star on his uniform. Munjed takes a deep breath as the officer flicks through the pages.

When the man finds the money, he slips it into a drawer and stamps their passports. Munjed is relieved but also shocked. Being part of this blatant bribery makes him feel sick. He desperately wants to turn around and leave. But where could he go?

He follows Hussein and Ali. They collect their bags then look for a phone booth. Munjed dials the number they've been given. A smuggler answers the phone and tells them where they need to go. They catch a taxi to a dilapidated hotel in a dirty rundown area on the waterfront north of Jakarta.

Munjed clutches his luggage. Besides a few clothes, his only companion from Iraq is a medical text called *Last's Anatomy* that he'd had with him when he escaped from the hospital that fateful day. Little does he know how much this book will bring him solace during the dark days ahead.

8

High seas without a skipper

The entrance to the dilapidated hotel is via a dim alley. Munjed fears he's made a terrible mistake. Over one thousand people are crammed into six storeys of human misery. The majority of the people are men from rural communities in Middle Eastern countries. They have very traditional attitudes and dress, which Munjed is not used to.

There are only a few women, including middle-aged Hoda, who is travelling with her nieces, Doha, Noor, Mary Anne and her nephew Ali. They wear Western clothes and have more relaxed attitudes.

Munjed is waiting beside another man in the foyer when Doha walks past wearing make-up and fashionable clothes. A burly young man scowls and mutters a threat. Munjed is horrified. The man's values are so different from those of his own moderate family.

He's also sickened by the behaviour of the people smugglers. They go about their illegal business freely, ignoring the terrible suffering around them. One smuggler drives an expensive Jeep and his boss has a new Mercedes. Police who must have been paid to turn a blind eye, loiter outside the hotel at all hours beside security guys armed with automatic weapons.

Ali, Munjed and Hussein move into rooms on the top floor of the hotel and are told to expect a long wait. Getting onto a boat going to Australia usually takes months, but when the smugglers realise that Munjed is a doctor, he is moved to the front of the queue.

'My prayers have been answered,' a smuggler with a big gold tooth tells him. 'I asked for a doctor to help with seasickness and a mullah to pray for the passengers. God has sent me both!'

He offers Munjed a place on a boat leaving almost immediately. There will be three heavily pregnant women on board. Munjed accepts the deal and asks that his companions leave with him. The smugglers refuse.

> **Mullah** is the name for an Islamic teacher or leader.

'I will not leave without Ali and Hussein,' Munjed insists. Grudgingly, the smugglers agree.

'What medical supplies will you need?'

'That depends on the size of the boat,' Munjed replies.

'It's a decent boat. I've just refitted the engine.'

'And how many people will be on board?'

'There will be 50 passengers, including the women who are pregnant.'

Munjed frowns. 'I'll need tablets and drugs to prevent seasickness and vomiting, cannulas, syringes, needles and at least 100 litres of saline fluid.'

'Okay,' Gold Tooth agrees. 'I'll get all that.'

A few days earlier when Munjed was listening to the news, he heard about a refugee boat that sank with no survivors. When he asks to see the boat they'll be travelling on, the Indonesian dealer is vague, but he does deliver the medical supplies. Later the gold-toothed man returns.

'I will take you and the mullah to see the boat,' he tells Munjed.

Getting there is a nightmare. The driver stays on back streets and keeps checking the rear mirror, clearly nervous. Munjed suspects Indonesian police, those who have not been paid off, are looking for this car.

They drive into a slum area near a dock. The smuggler points to an old fishing boat with blue flaking paint. It's about 15 metres long with a single deck and one small covered area towards the back. The boat reeks of fish and there's another smell that's worse. Munjed follows his nose and sees a 60-centimetre hole in the deck – the toilet! A bucket sits beside it.

'This boat is way too small for 50 people,' he objects.

Inshallah is an Arabic expression meaning: *God willing.*

'Everyone will fit,' Gold Tooth growls. 'No problem.'

'*Inshallah,*' the mullah adds, as he blesses the boat.

Munjed thinks they'll need a lot more than blessings, but he pays the smuggler $ 2000 as there are no better options. He's determined to reach a safe haven or die trying.

They return to the hotel and prepare to leave early the next morning. Meanwhile the fishing boat sets sail for a secret pick-up location. At 7a.m. the asylum seekers gather. A mixture of excitement and anxiety fills the room.

'Take one small bag of belongings and a passport,' Gold Tooth tells them all, 'and definitely no other documents.'

Munjed makes sure he packs his prized possession, the dog-eared *Last's Anatomy*. Before they leave, he revises what he knows about late-term pregnancy.

> In **late-term pregnancy,** a woman can expect:
> - Her organs to have shifted around to make room for the growing baby.
> - Her heart size to increase as it needs to supply oxygenated blood to the foetus.
> - Her uterus to grow from the size of a flattened pear to the size of a small watermelon.
> - Her feet could increase a size.
> - To have a heightened sense of smell.

Remembering the boat's fishy stench and simple toilet, all he can think is, *I'm glad I'm not a pregnant woman.*

A bus arrives and 50 people crowd aboard. The bus looks even less reliable than the painted-headlights-bus that took the Al Muderis family from Amman to Baghdad all those years ago. After almost 24 hours of driving, they reach their destination and the driver says, 'Okay, we are here,' but then he suddenly turns the bus around. When this happens a second time, Munjed thinks the driver must be dodging police.

At dusk they disembark at last and the smugglers soon pull up in their expensive cars. They're accompanied by guards with automatic guns which Munjed has no doubt they'll happily use.

Two more buses turn up with another hundred or so people. Surely, they can't *all* be leaving on the same boat. Munjed is now very nervous and angry. The boat was not big enough for 50 people, and now there are three times that number. Again, it is too late for any of them to change their minds and none of them have a better choice anyway.

The refugees are taken to a sandy bay where the fishing boat is moored in shallow water. Everything is dark and still. Suddenly, a spotlight shines onto the beach and a human shuttle begins. It takes hours for one small dinghy to ferry dozens of small groups out to the boat.

The women go first. Hoda's youngest niece, 13-year-old Mary Anne, is wearing shorts and a Tweety bird t-shirt. Her clothing infuriates the mullah. As Mary Anne climbs into the tinnie, he raises his arms.

'If this girl goes aboard, the boat will sink!'

The already terrified people panic. Munjed clenches his fists and it takes all his wits to talk down the fiery-eyed mullah.

'We cannot split a family,' Munjed reasons. 'This child must not be separated from her loved ones.'

The mullah grumbles and backs down. Mary Anne scrambles aboard and all the women, including the pregnant ones, squeeze into the tiny sheltered area at the back of the boat.

Next, it's the men's turn to board. Free-for-all shoving breaks out. In the madness, one fellow has a seizure. Before leaving Iran, this man was said to be a member of the vicious Badr Brigade, a ruthless group of torturers. If that's true he should not be on this boat seeking asylum as he's *not* a refugee.

Munjed saves the man's life, but he'll come to regret it in the months ahead.

Conditions on board the tiny fishing boat are appalling. There's no room to sit, so people stand, crammed together like sardines, on the open deck. The boat has no evacuation plan, no emergency beacons and just a few life jackets ... for 165 people, most of whom can't swim. As for the crew, a skinny Indonesian fisherman captains the boat, with the help of two teenagers aged around twelve and fourteen.

Munjed finds a place on the canopy over the rear part of the deck where others are too scared to go. He has a little more room there, but if there are medical emergencies, he has no idea how he'll get across the crowded boat to treat them.

'*Ayo pergi,*' the captain tells his teenage helpers, 'let's go'.

As the fisherman starts the engine, Munjed realises his chances of surviving this trip to Australia are extremely slim. There's no doubt they're in for a horror journey, but if they do reach safety, any suffering will be worth it. He grips his treasured anatomy book as they head off to the unknown in the flimsiest of craft.

Most people seeking asylum in Australia arrive by air and not by boat. **Asylum seekers** who arrive by boat are more likely to be **refugees** who need to flee rapidly and do not have time to arrange travel through authorised channels. It is also dangerous for them to apply for a passport or exit visa as this could put their lives, and the lives of their families, at risk.

The waves become choppy as they leave the sheltered harbour. Many of the people have never seen the ocean or been in a boat before. Cries of *Allah Akhbar* (God is great) are accompanied by moans of terror. Waves slap the hull. People begin vomiting and because they're so tightly packed, they vomit onto each other. This starts a chain reaction. Soon everyone is vomiting. As they lose fluids, Munjed does what he can to rehydrate them. Then people lose control of their bladders. The smell of urine and vomit overwhelms him.

A boat which looks like an Indonesian naval frigate escorts the fishing boat out to sea, but as soon as they reach international waters, a black dinghy from the frigate pulls aside the fishing boat. The Indonesian skipper jumps into the dinghy.

'Stay on a straight course,' he yells to the sick and horrified refugees, as he heads to the safety of the larger vessel. 'In about 30 hours you will reach Christmas Island.'

The lives of 165 desperate people now lie in the hands of two nervous teenagers. People start shouting and crying.

'Come back!'

'Don't leave us...'

A tall Iraqi man steps forward.

'I have served in the navy back home,' he says. 'I'm not a master mariner but I will do what I can to help.'

While the man navigates, Munjed treats sick passengers on the overcrowded deck. Hussein and Ali have no medical training but they pass syringes and help him insert saline drips.

The next part of the journey is a blur of churning seas, crashing waves and the putrid smell of desperate people. At some point it rains, a light shower at first, which builds into a soaking downpour. Huge waves toss the boat. People flop about the deck, falling across each other like dying fish.

After twelve hours the medical supplies run out. One man is in a coma, another is close to death. Munjed has kept the last anti-nausea drugs for the pregnant women. Thankfully, none of them goes into early labour.

The rain continues all night.

'How can I navigate without stars?' the Iraqi sailor mutters. In the wretched darkness Munjed hears prayers and terrified sobbing.

The refugees were told the journey would be 30 to 40 hours. As the nightmare continues, Munjed's greatest fear is that they will miss their target and sail straight past Christmas Island to Antarctica. At dawn on the second day the wind drops and the rain eases. The ocean becomes calm. They drift onwards, people moaning, vomiting and toileting where they stand. The sun beats down on them all. The stench is unbearable.

About 7p.m., Munjed and the sailor see lights. They stare as the glow disappears and reappears, reluctant to announce a false sighting and raise everyone's hopes. After about 20 minutes they're sure. Relief floods through Munjed's body.

They've survived.

Navigation is no longer a problem – they simply head for the lights. After 36 harrowing hours, they can see the rocky shores of Christmas Island. Two kilometres from the island, the Australian Federal Police intercept them.

'Stop! Where are you from?'

'We are asylum seekers.'

The police come aboard. Munjed's knees suddenly feel weak. He's made it.

The federal agents – two men and one woman – are clearly horrified by the conditions. They wear gloves but not masks and, despite their best efforts, the smell makes them dry retch.

'Come off the boat,' they say in kind voices. 'Do not take any belongings. We'll bring them to you later.'

It's 8 November, 1999. Munjed is lucky to be one of the first to step ashore. As his feet touch land, he wobbles about on unsteady legs.

'Everything will be okay now,' he whispers, thinking of the friends and family who risked their lives to help him escape.

Little does he know...

9

You are not welcome

Christmas Island is 360 kilometres south of Java in the Indian Ocean, but 1,400 kilometres from Australia's northern coast. The air is humid and Munjed can hear strange birds calling. Although the Federal Police are efficient, it takes hours to process 165 people. Photos are taken of each asylum seeker then they're given a number and tagged with a hospital-like bracelet. Doha and Munjed are the only English speakers so they stay behind to help translate. This means they're the last to be processed.

Police officers take the asylum seekers to a makeshift camp in a basketball stadium, where they're given fresh clothes and a towel from The Salvation Army. Everyone is desperate to wash, but there are only three showers, so Munjed waits for hours. When it's his turn, he sighs in relief as the warm shower washes away days of filth. Then he has to line up for food.

For a while the stadium is mayhem. The local takeaway restaurant has gone into overdrive and is sending batches of rice with honey chicken wings as quickly as they can make it. The mixture of sweet and sour is weird for Munjed's tastebuds, but he's ravenous and grateful to wolf it down.

Once everyone is clean and fed, people relax. Their chatter fills the basketball court, reminding Munjed of a busy indoor market at home.

'Number One,' the police call as they start interviewing the asylum seekers. Munjed offers to help again. They don't finish until the early hours of the morning. When all the details are recorded Munjed settles down on a thin yoga mattress and sleeps deeply.

In the morning the new arrivals are offered cornflakes, toast, jam and tea with milk and sugar. The mullah and some others are not satisfied with this.

'Please thank the authorities for the breakfast,' the mullah tells Munjed, 'but say that we would like the kind of food we are used to'.

Munjed is gobsmacked and ashamed by this ungrateful attitude. The Australians have been generous in a challenging situation. He walks away from the mullah and doesn't bother passing on his message.

After dinner on the second night the processing continues.

During breaks, Munjed inhales warm salty air mixed with the fragrance of tropical plants. Looking up at the incredibly clear blue sky, he is filled with anticipation. He can't wait to start a new life in this beautiful country. He'll work hard, hone his medical skills and soon be able to help those in need.

'Enjoy it while you're here,' a police officer warns him. 'The place where they'll be taking you next is not somewhere you'll want to stay for long.'

Munjed frowns. Everyone has been so kind; surely things will not be too different on the mainland.

On the third day the police organise a soccer game.

'Pass it here,' Munjed yells and his team cheers as he scores a goal. How long since he's felt this relaxed and optimistic!

One fellow falls and injures his ankle. Munjed helps the doctor treat him at the local hospital. On the way back to the basketball stadium, the doctor takes him for a tour.

The island colours are striking: the very blue sky, the very lush, green forests, and surprisingly, millions of very red crabs! Munjed learns that the asylum seekers have arrived on the island during the annual crab migration.

For most of the year the huge red crabs live in the island's tropical forests. Then at the beginning of the wet season, millions of them head for the sea. They follow the same migration path every year, climbing over anything and everything on their way to the coast. This lasts for about two weeks.

As the doctor shows Munjed the sights, their car wheels crunch over the crabs crossing the road.

'Sorry, mate,' the doctor says. 'There's no way to go around them.'

NORTH SOUTH BASELINE   AIRPORT · IRVINE HILL RD

IRVINE HILL RD

TOWNSHIP

DON'T DRIVE OVER   ROBBER CRABS !

SLOWLY   SAFELY

...DRIVE AROUND THEM EVEN IN 4WD'S

Red crabs

• Red crabs, or *Gecarcoidea natalis* are only found on Christmas Island and Cocos (Keeling) Islands.

• The migration begins with the males furthest from shore heading from the forests to the coast. Other crabs join them.

• After mating, the males head back to the forest while the females stay in the burrows to brood their eggs. This can take a couple of weeks.

• The females deposit their ripe eggs into the ocean and head back to the forest. The eggs hatch into larvae and then tiny prawn-like animals called megalops. After four weeks they leave the sea and moult into baby crabs.

'Where are they going?'

'Down to the sea to spawn. Their body clocks are amazing. The migration always happens on the last quarter moon before the wet season.'

Crunch, crunch, crunch.

Munjed winces, thinking about the opening scene in *The Terminator* when the giant truck drives over a mountain of skulls. He remembers Ismail laughing at the nude cyborg and wonders what his cousin is doing now.

Crunch, crunch.

'No one knows how many there are,' the doctor continues, 'but most people say at least 50 or maybe even 100 million. This type of crab is only found here and on the Cocos Islands, about 900 kilometres southwest of here.'

What a strange and beautiful place, Munjed thinks.

Back at the basketball stadium, Munjed and the others are ushered out to the barbeque area.

'Watch this,' a police officer says. 'We have a flaming big sign to mark the end of your voyage.'

The refugees peer though the wire fence and see their rickety fishing boat anchored in the bay. The police have loaded explosives onto it.

Bang!

Munjed watches wreckage fly into the air as the boat detonates. 'There's no going back now,' he laughs.

'Right, now that's done,' the policeman says, 'let's have a game of volleyball'.

The officers join the asylum seekers in a friendly game. There are good players and not-so-good players on both sides, but everyone joins in. Sport unites people from all backgrounds, Munjed thinks. His experience with the federal police on Christmas Island is so positive.

Another boat arrives and the next morning Munjed is asked to translate again. They go to meet the asylum seekers in two boats. Some police officers are in one small barge and Munjed is with another in the second barge.

'Does your family know where you are?' the officer asks.

'No,' Munjed replies. 'We're not allowed to use the phones.'

The officer reaches into his pocket and holds out a satellite phone.

'Call your mum,' he says.

'What?' Munjed stares. The last time he spoke to his mother was the night before they left Jakarta.

'I'm taking a huge risk,' the man continues. 'If you tell anyone about this, I'll lose my job.' Munjed thanks him and quickly makes the call. Luckily, Kamila is home.

'Mama, it's me,' Munjed says. 'I'm in Australia and I'm safe.'

Kamila can barely speak through her tears. 'My son, I've been so worried—'

After hearing reports of boats sinking at sea, Kamila is beside herself with relief.

'I can only speak for a few seconds,' Munjed interrupts. 'Everything is okay, but I will be going into detention. You might not hear from me for a while.'

'Alright, I understand.'

'I have to go now, Mama. I love you.'

'I love you, too. Stay safe.'

He hands the phone back and says, 'How can I ever repay you?'

The officer smiles. 'No worries, mate. Just pass it on.'

Munjed feels as if he is back on the spinning wheel of fortune. He's survived a terrible journey organised by greedy profiteers and has now received a generous act of kindness. The unknown man's compassion teaches Munjed a valuable life lesson: when you have a chance to help a fellow human, do it. You may not get a second chance. He vows to repay this good deed a hundred times over once his fortune changes again, as he's sure it will. He knows not to *expect* good outcomes, but to value them when they *do* arrive. And to be prepared, strong and ready for when the wheel turns downwards.

They reach the refugee boat. It's smaller than the Indonesian fishing boat but better equipped. There are fewer than 40 people aboard, many of them children. Everyone looks exhausted. These asylum seekers are Vietnamese so Munjed is unable to translate. The police help the Vietnamese ashore and they all return to the stadium. These new arrivals are separated from the others by a rope in case they're sick and infect each other. The groups are just a metre apart. As a doctor, Munjed knows this is absurd.

Many of the asylum seekers spend the day chatting, but being idle frustrates Munjed. He flicks through his anatomy book whenever he can, thinking, I may as well use this in-between time to study. He tests himself on some of the things he's experiencing.

Munjed's symptoms

- **Sweating:** Helps release heat, which maintains optimal body temperature.
- **Anxiety:** When your *body* responds to danger, you breathe rapidly because your lungs are trying to move more oxygen through your *body* in case you need to escape or protect yourself. This is called the fight-or-flight response.

After five days on the island, the final group from Munjed's boat is flown to Curtin Detention Centre in a small commercial jet. The friendly federal police officers hand over the care of the asylum seekers to grim-faced guards from Australasian Correctional Management (ACM). The worst part of Munjed's ordeal is about to begin.

They land at a remote airbase and taxi across the tarmac. When the pilot kills the engines, the air-conditioning dies too. The heat in the plane is stifling. If anyone tries to stand or ask a question the ACM guards bark abuse. Munjed remembers the police officer's warning – 'The place where they'll be taking you is not somewhere you'll want to stay for long'. He is filled with foreboding.

After almost an hour of waiting a bus arrives.

'Everyone out!' the guards shout.

They drive across a desolate landscape towards shed-like buildings behind a tall wire fence that is topped with razor wire. The dirt is brownish red with clumps of scraggly bushes here and there. Their bus enters the gates and Munjed sees people lining the access road.

As they get out of the bus the other detainees hold out photos.

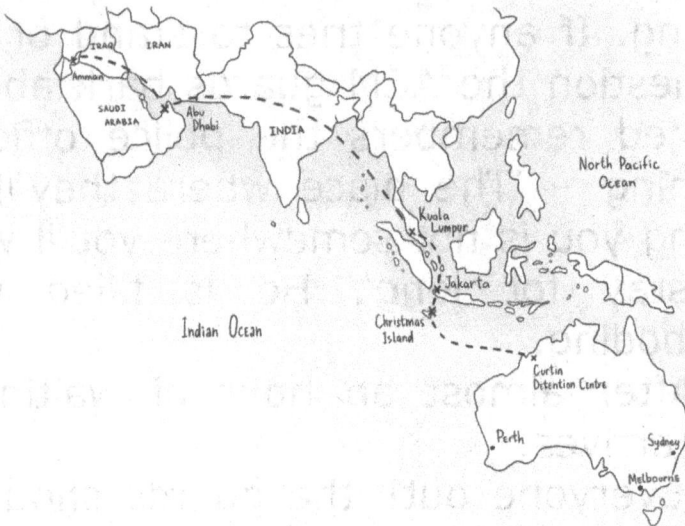

'Was my wife, Sadaf, on your boat?'

'Have you seen my son? His name is Farokh.'

'Do you know if my brother is alive? He is tall and walks with a limp.'

'Where did you leave from? My family stayed at a hotel near Jakarta. Perhaps you met them?'

The desperation and misery is palpable. One man stands alone.

'Why did you come here?' he whispers. 'It's awful.'

Munjed looks into the man's desperate eyes and shivers.

10

1999/2000: #982

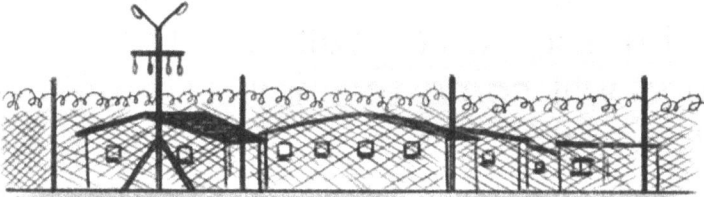

Munjed soon comes to appreciate the warning of the federal police officer on Christmas Island. The basketball stadium there was a tropical paradise compared to the hellhole of Curtin Detention Centre, which lays hidden in Western Australia's remote Kimberley region, 30 kilometres from the nearest town of Derby.

Upon arrival, Munjed is issued the number 982. A guard writes it on Munjed's wrist and shoulder in permanent black marker. He feels like a branded animal. Being stripped of his name and called by a number is the most demeaning thing anyone has ever done to him.

Buildings sprawl across the red dirt and detainees are crammed into tents with about 20 beds in each. There are six compounds separated from each other called Alpha, Bravo, Charlie, Delta, Echo and Foxtrot. There's also a punishment unit called 'The Hotel'. Munjed will come to know this unit well.

The detainees are given no change of clothing or protection from the blazing heat and their bags are taken away from them and placed in storage, as if they were in jail. All they're allowed is a toothbrush, toothpaste, thongs and a towel.

As he's being processed, one of the guards taunts, 'Don't try and escape because the nearest town is a long way and you'll die of thirst!'

Seeking asylum is actually not illegal, yet Munjed and others are treated like criminals. The detainees who've come by boat are often called '**queue jumpers**' by people who don't understand that there is, in fact, no 'queue' for many asylum seekers.

They're also told that the Kimberley is home to many poisonous creatures.

'Be careful,' a guard tells Munjed. 'If the snakes or spiders bite you, then you can die in just a few minutes.' The guard laughs as he walks away. Munjed wonders what sort of person takes such pleasure in another's misfortune.

Soon after their arrival, a woman from the Department of Immigration addresses the asylum seekers. They gather around a loudspeaker to listen, wondering what will happen to them and how they'll get to the next stage of their journey to a new life.

'You're not welcome here,' she says in a cold voice. 'The Australian people do not want you here. You could be detained for a long time and there is no guarantee that you will be allowed to stay in this country. However, if you choose to go back to your homeland, we can help organise that.'

Munjed cannot believe what he is hearing. He didn't know that the government had just changed the law and that it was now much more difficult for people to seek asylum in Australia – particularly if they came on a boat.

The worst part of being in Curtin is the guards. Most treat the asylum seekers with little respect, as if they're not even human. Munjed is shocked to see how cruel and violent they can be. In the weeks ahead he will see regular beatings and terrible bullying.

There is an international agreement called the Refugee Convention, which Australia has signed in 1951, along with most other nations. If a person comes to Australia as a refugee, the Immigration Department checks to see if your story is true before you are allowed to stay. That's why Munjed and the others are put into a detention centre.

***

For months the detainees receive no information. Many lose hope. They don't know when (or even *if*) they will be processed.

> The **Department of Immigration** researches your background, your family, what's happening in your country and whether it is too dangerous for you to remain there.

> This is what is meant by 'processing' the refugees.

The hot dusty days stretch forever, fuelling despair, frustration and anger. This leads to fights and violence. Like his father, Munjed is a natural peacemaker, so he speaks out when he sees injustice. But this gets him into trouble, especially with the camp commander, who takes an instant dislike to Munjed.

The guards yell abuse at the asylum seekers for the slightest reason. They mock them and call out racist insults. There are endless threats of violence.

It's the children Munjed feels most sorry for. Some of them have no family or friends – they're on their own, scared and vulnerable. And even the youngest child at Curtin is known only by a number.

'Hey, 329, come over here,' the guards shout, or, 'Get back inside, 275!'

***

Munjed is afraid the little ones will be traumatised for life. He spends hours teaching English to the younger detainees, giving them (and him) some distraction during the endless days. If the children do get to stay in Australia, they'll need English to settle in and make new friends.

There are lots of things at the centre that seem unfair. For instance, even though it's extremely hot, each mealtime everyone has to line up for hours in the scorching sun. Breakfast is *always* cornflakes, toast, jam and tea. And lunch and dinner are *always* mincemeat and spaghetti with either an apple or an orange. Only at Easter, do they get a boiled egg as a treat.

Some people smuggle extra toast back to their tent but that attracts ants and other creatures. One morning a detainee finds a snake in his tent which he kills. But that gets him into trouble.

'You stupid idiot,' a guard roars. 'That snake is a protected species.'

How was the man to know that? Munjed wonders, when the guards here have said the snakes are deadly. He sighs. Snakes in this country seem to have more value than human asylum seekers.

Detainees are not allowed to have cups, even plastic ones, so each time Munjed wants a drink he has to walk to a communal tap and drink directly from it. The problem is that every night from 7p.m. until 7a.m., just like in prisons, the centre has lockdown. No matter how thirsty Munjed becomes during the hot nights, he cannot go and get a drink.

And worse than in prison, the guards wake everyone at midnight, shining a torch into their faces to check their identity. This causes problems for the women who feel embarrassed and dishonoured to be seen by a man when they're not fully dressed.

The boredom is unbearable. There are no newspapers or magazines. No

TV. No radio. No phones. Munjed longs for a chess set to practise his moves, but that's forbidden also. One man, who will later become a respected Sydney obstetrician, spends the day pacing the perimeter fence, like a caged animal.

Over time, some guards get to know the detainees and become more sympathetic. After hours of badgering one of the friendlier ones, Munjed is finally allowed to have his anatomy book. He spends hours reading it from cover to cover. When he's not studying, he carves shapes into the concrete blocks that hold up his tent poles. It passes the time for a while.

With nothing to do, arguments break out between different groups and there's even a riot over cigarettes. Many detainees are addicted to nicotine. When their allowance of three cigarettes a day is stopped, they become angry. Munjed tries to act as a peacemaker, but without any luck. The guards film the disturbance and instead of seeing him as someone who is trying to stop the fighting, they accuse him of being a ringleader. They handcuff him and take him to the lockup at Derby Police Station for a few days.

In January 2000, frustration with processing delays and inhumane treatment boils over. The asylum seekers plan a hunger strike. After a week of unrest Doha, Munjed and a few others are allowed to form a committee. They bring suggestions to the authorities on ways to make the detainees' lives more bearable. This leads to better conditions.

A classroom is opened where detainees can learn basic English and receive lessons about Australian culture. Doha's aunt volunteers to work in the kitchen to improve the meals. People are also allowed to write letters and watch television.

But not all the changes are positive. There are some very conservative detainees who see Munjed and his committee as enemies. One of them is a menacing fellow called Al Sayed. There are rumours that he was once part of Saddam Hussein's brutal Secret Intelligence Service, and that he organised many assassinations. Al Sayed is able to create an intimidating rule of terror within the camp. And he also gains recognition and influence with some of the camp authorities.

The detainees are reaching the end of their tether and they're desperate to know when this will all end. One day, Munjed learns that the Immigration Minister, Phillip Ruddock, is planning a secret visit. Munjed asks whether he could meet with him. He wants to tell Mr Ruddock about their conditions and to ask the minister how long it will be for their requests for asylum to be processed.

He's told that a meeting is not possible.

Munjed knows this could be their only chance to find a way out of this terrible place. So they organise a demonstration. Asylum seekers make banners from their sheets with messages protesting against the lack of processing. When the Minister arrives, 1,000 detainees march peacefully across the camp.

The camp manager is furious! But the committee *is* allowed to meet the Minister.

'What do you want?' Philip Ruddock demands in a frosty voice.

'To know why your government spends so much money each day to keep us here when we could be tagged and allowed to do something useful like working on a farm.'

'That will never happen.'

Munjed tries again. 'When will our applications be processed?' he asks.

The minister replies that it will take as long as needed.

'If you want to go back to where you came from,' he adds, 'the government can organise that immediately'.

11

Still waiting

Time drags on and on. Still the detainees hear nothing about whether they can stay in Australia. Violent incidents become more common. The guards continue to humiliate the detainees. Everyone is on edge.

As desperation increases, divisions between groups worsen. Some people are bashed, others disappear into solitary confinement. The fundamentalists cause trouble in many ways. One example is their abusive language to Doha and her sisters, telling them they must cover their hair. They also insist on marking a holy day with self-mutilation rituals. Beds are smashed for metal rods. Then the fundamentalists gather in the yard to cry and beat themselves.

'Stop,' Munjed tells them, 'Your behaviour will reflect badly on everyone.'

They ignore him.

Shortly afterwards Munjed is marched to the main office. The fundamentalists, including the scary Al Sayed, are already there.

'Squat on the floor with the others,' a guard orders.

Munjed does as he is told.

'Here he is,' one of the men smirks. 'The one who organised this disturbance.'

No one listens when Munjed says it's not true. The men, including Munjed, are herded into a van and taken to Derby Police Station where they're locked in two concrete cells which smell of vomit and stale sweat. A steel toilet with no privacy sits in the corner. All that Munjed is given to sleep on is a towel.

They're kept in the police cells all night and the next day. Even when the cell heats up in the fiercely hot desert sun, they're only allowed out for one hour to exercise.

At last a representative from the Immigration Department arrives.

'You've been brought here to teach you a lesson,' he says to Munjed. 'Will you promise to stop what you were doing and behave?'

Munjed knows the manager of the detention centre does not like him and that he's been marked as 'a troublemaker'. Although he has no idea what he's being accused of, he agrees to 'behave'.

When they get back to the centre, all of the detainees have been crammed onto one side of the camp. Processing is going to begin. At last! They start with the first numbers but because Munjed stayed back to help translate on arrival at Christmas Island, # 982 will be one of the last.

Processing is ad hoc. Anyone who says they're from Iraq gets a visa even though Munjed is pretty sure many are actually from Iran. After ten days, most detainees have been moved to the other side of the compound, including his friends Ali, Hussein, Doha and her family.

> **Ad hoc** means something is not planned; it happens as needed or requested.

But Munjed's number is never called.

'What's happening?' he asks the guards.

They shrug. No one bothers to answer his questions.

Then the immigration officials leave.

Munjed has been deliberately left out. Almost everyone else in the camp has some hope of being accepted into Australia, while he remains in limbo at the detention centre. Unless he is interviewed, Munjed can't be accepted or rejected. He is devastated. There are no glasses to be half-full. He hangs his head and stares at the red dust, trying to make sense of this injustice.

Meanwhile, restrictions are relaxed for the other asylum seekers who have been accepted as refugees. Telephone lines are installed, and detainees are paid to do jobs around the centre like cleaning the toilets, cooking and doing odd jobs. Most importantly, they can talk to their loved ones outside the centre.

For Munjed nothing changes.

He has no name, no rights and no one seems to care. He's become invisible.

Months earlier, a nurse had suggested that Munjed write down everything that was happening in the detention centre.

'Showing photographs would be even better,' Munjed replied. So, the nurse smuggled in a camera. Then he sent Munjed's bleak images to media outlets across Australia. No newspaper published them. No one was interested.

As Munjed waits to be processed, it seems they are still not interested.

Then the wheel of fortune turns and a random act of kindness helps him. A sympathetic guard smuggles Munjed into the telephone area, so he can call his mum.

'Mama!'

'Munjed, is it really you?' Kamila is thrilled to hear her son's voice for the first time in six months, but very distressed by his situation. 'Why haven't you called?'

After quickly explaining, Munjed says, 'I need an immigration agent to put forward my case with the authorities.'

'Don't worry. Leave it to me...'

This determined woman has already saved Munjed's life once and she's ready to do so again. She contacts a Sydney immigration agent.

Suddenly, Munjed has an advocate. Dr Al Jabiri calls the Immigration Department. He gives them Munjed's number and says he wants to speak with his client. This causes an uproar.

'How did you make contact with this man?' the detention staff demand.

Munjed doesn't say – there's no way he's going to dob in the kind guard who helped him.

Now he can be interviewed like everyone else, but the pace of processing is still very slow. Some of the detainees begin to worry that they'll be locked up for another year. They steal cutting implements and one night they slice through the perimeter fence. Over 100 people surge though, but there is no way Munjed is going to join them. He doesn't want to be falsely accused of being involved again.

The breakout is short-lived because it's easy for the police to block the one road into town. They gather the escapees and bring them back.

A few days later, Munjed's fears are realised. Even though he had made sure that was well away from the breakout, the management of the centre accuse him of organising it. Munjed suspects the fundamentalists and ex-Badr soldier he helped in Indonesia are behind the accusation. They hope that if they can point the finger at Munjed for organising the unrest, their visas will be processed faster.

When guards march Munjed to a federal police officer, he says, 'You are charged with inciting people to break out of the detention centre.'

'I had nothing to do with it,' Munjed protests. But the officer refuses to believe him.

Yet again he is taken to the Derby Police Station, where he is fingerprinted and photographed. From there he is driven 220 kilometres to Broome and locked in the Maximum Security Prison. The wheel of fortune is spinning out of control.

This time he is sharing a cell with a man charged with murder and another facing drug charges. The conditions are much better in jail than the detention centre. Here the food is brilliant (although he's handcuffed to cross the yard to get it), he can use the phones, watch TV and even use a pool table.

He teaches the alleged murderer chess, and in return, learns about the man's culture. But the best part is that the guards call Munjed by his name, *not* a number. He feels human again.

After a few days in Broome, Munjed is escorted to another prison. This time it's in Karratha, 830 kilometres south of Broome. The journey takes twelve hours. For the whole time, he's stuck inside a non-air-conditioned truck with small windows and a toilet in the middle. The smell is horrible and the heat is unbearable!

When Munjed arrives at Karratha prison he's happy to discover that it's even better than Broome. He has his own cell, a bed with clean sheets and his own toilet. And, even more luxurious, he can shower whenever he wants. But the best thing of all is that there is a library.

Munjed uses his time to study and to write letters to Amnesty International and the media. He also contacts a solicitor in Perth who becomes another advocate for him. Between all of this, he plays football and watches kangaroos hop around the outside of the jail.

Amnesty International is a non-government organisation that defends human rights and works to change oppressive or unjust laws.

After a week he's taken back to Broome. The charge against him is, luckily, heard by a magistrate who seems to have some knowledge of what people at the detention centre are really like, so despite intimidating stares from the camp guards, the case against Munjed is thrown out. There's applause and cheers from people watching in the courtroom gallery, including some of the police officers.

However, it's not over yet. Munjed's first night back at Curtin Detention Centre is spent in isolation. He has no idea why. His cell is two metres by two metres. It has no windows and there is only a thin mattress on the floor with no pillow. A bright fluorescent light is on 24 hours a day and a camera in the ceiling records his every move.

'What's going on?' Munjed asks the guards on the second evening. 'Why am I being kept here?'

They don't reply.

A day later, an officer tells him, 'After spending time with criminals, we're rehabilitating you.'

Munjed suspects the real reason is that the camp manager was furious when the magistrate dismissed his case.

While Munjed is locked in the punishment unit, others who he believes have lied about their back ground are being processed. Injustice eats at him. He's paid a heavy price for speaking out, for trying to improve conditions for all the detainees and for trying to get the processing happening.

For the first time in his life, Munjed feels like giving up.

Our brains can play tricks on us if we're locked up in isolation without a window and with a light on all the time. Munjed doesn't know when it's day or night, or how many days have gone by. With no one to talk to, childhood memories start to drift through his mind.

He remembers the beautiful leafy Green Zone of Baghdad and his mother's lush garden, filled with date palms and citrus trees laden with lemons and oranges. He pictures the Tigris River snaking through the city, and remembers happy evenings when the Al Muderis family strolled by the waterside restaurants.

He swats a bug.

Those evening lights were so pretty. He is walking along the leafy riverbank with his mother. They stop at playgrounds and cafes to meet friends, then drive home in his mother's MG sports car.

Munjed touches his head, remembering the feeling of wind in his hair. Then he opens his eyes, the images of the beautiful streets of Baghdad fading as he looks around the dirty room. Tears fill his eyes. In his solitary cell only the camera sees them fall.

By the third day, Munjed refuses to eat.

The manager visits him then.

'What do you want now?' he asks.

'To be in the main compound.'

'You could be at risk of self-harm or be attacked by other detainees. That's why you're in solitary confinement.'

Munjed knows the man is lying.

'I won't eat or drink until I know what is really going on,' he replies.

'God, you're a pain,' he sneers.

The only change is that Doha is allowed to visit. Then Munjed is transferred from solitary to the punishment wing.

'Welcome to The Hotel,' a guard grins.

This is where Munjed will spend his last 40 days at the detention centre. Some of the guards are friendly and are happy to play chess with him. There's also time for him to read *Last's Anatomy* from cover-to-cover several times.

In August 2000, Munjed is finally granted asylum. # 982 is free, but the Detention Camp Manager has one final act of cruelty. While other detainees are transferred to a city of their choice, Munjed is told he'll have to organise his own travel.

'You have money and good English,' the manager says. 'I'll get one of the officers to take you to the main road. There'll be a bus coming from Derby around six o'clock tomorrow morning. It'll take you to Broome.'

Curtin Detention Centre is about 200 kilometres north east of Broome, and Broome to Perth is a distance of 2,230 kilometres – a three-day bus ride. The bus from Perth to Melbourne, where Munjed has decided to go, takes several more days. It's 3,460 kilometres from Perth.

Brutes come in all shapes and sizes. Munjed has been dealing with bullies since he was small, some of whom carried assault rifles. In comparison the Detention Centre Manager is small fry. Using his glass half-full mantra, Munjed sees the journey as an opportunity to learn about his new home.

A month before the 2000 Sydney Olympics, Munjed stands outside the Curtin Detention Centre.

He turns his back on the barbed wire fence, squints into the glare and waits for the bus.

Munjed is in excellent spirits as he sets out on the 5,700-kilometre road journey to Melbourne. He's excited to see parts of the country that many Australians may never have even heard of. Most of all, he is keen to put as many kilometres as possible between him and the hated detention centre.

Curtin Detention Centre was established in 1999 by the Howard government. An inquiry in 2001 found chronic overcrowding, poor staff training, racial abuse and inadequate facilities for children.

It closed in 2002 after ongoing rioting. The facility has since been described as, 'the worst of Australia's hellholes'.

The Centre was reopened in 2010 by the Rudd/Gillard government and was used until 2014.

12

2001: Survival of the fittest

Kamila mails her son a copy of his medical degree, but while he is waiting to be registered to work as a doctor in Australia, he finds a job cleaning toilets. For Munjed, doing any work is an honour, so he's happy to scrub toilet bowls while he waits for a medical posting.

After his registration comes through, he sends out 100 résumés to hospitals around the country. Finally, he lands a position as a junior doctor in the emergency department at Mildura Base Hospital in country Victoria.

Munjed is very proud that he only receives Centrelink payments for two months before becoming an Australian taxpayer. He tries to repay the money, but Centrelink won't accept it.

'There's a belief that as a refugee I'm the exception,' Munjed says, 'but out of 1,252 people who were with me in Curtin, 13 were doctors and 12 of those are now practising medical specialists in Australia'.

Munjed works hard in Mildura then relocates to the Austin Hospital in Melbourne, where he is offered a position as a surgical registrar. He's now one step closer to reaching his long-term goal of becoming an orthopaedic surgeon.

Although his new job has a huge workload, Munjed throws his energies into building his career. He receives accreditation in the Australian medical system and passes the initial exam for the Royal Australasian College of Surgeons. Although he remains optimistic, there are still more hurdles to jump.

Some doctors have been welcoming towards him but others are definitely not. That's something he did not expect. At one medical conference, he hears two surgeons say, 'Isn't it a shame that Australian orthopaedic standards have slipped so low that we allow refugees to become one of us...'

But instead of intimidating him, this comment only makes Munjed even more determined to excel.

'Thank you for waking me up,' he mutters. 'I'll show you what this refugee can do!'

Munjed has never lost sight of his teenage aspirations to find better solutions for amputees. Some of his fellow surgeons are sceptical of his ideas but Munjed, like a good chess player, focuses on the long game and takes inspiration from the words of Garry Kasparov, a Russian chess grandmaster: 'One does not succeed by sticking to convention'.

Munjed accepts a position as an orthopaedic registrar at Wollongong Hospital. He spends two years at Wollongong where three wonderful surgeons mentor him. After overcoming hardship and making it this far, his glass is becoming more full than empty.

The wheel of fortune turns upwards again when, in 2006, he is able to bring his mother to Australia.

As she comes through the international arrivals door at Melbourne Airport, there are tears of joy and sadness. They have not seen each other for seven years and after so much hardship and time apart, their reunion is bittersweet.

***

Between medical commitments Munjed does what he can to help other asylum seekers by speaking to the media about conditions at Curtin Detention Centre. He has a practical suggestion for how the Immigration Department could treat asylum seekers more humanely. Instead of locking people up while they're waiting to be processed, he suggests they could wear an electronic tag and live in a town or city where they could work. That would also save the government money, as detention centres cost millions of dollars to run.

'I'm sure they would be happy to pick fruit and learn the language and culture,' he says. 'They could report to a police station and, if necessary, stay in home-detention at night.'

Munjed calculates that keeping him in Curtin for so long cost taxpayers tens of thousands of dollars. He believes the money could have been better spent training asylum seekers in trades that are needed in Australia, like nursing or plumbing.

During the 1990s, surgeons had begun trialling osseointegration implants for above-knee amputees. The thrill Munjed got from watching Arnold Schwarzenegger rampage as a cyborg Terminator has never faded and he is still fascinated by robotics. What was once the stuff of fantasy is now possible and he wants to be at the forefront of this exciting technology. So in 2009, he moves to Berlin to research osseointegration techniques and complete postgraduate work in knee and hip replacement surgery.

Later the same year when he returns home, Munjed gathers a team of medical specialists. His dream of forming an Australian integrated osseointegration team is almost a reality.

Osseointegration began as an idea in the 1950s when a Swedish physician, Per-Ingvar Branemark, found that human bone can integrate with titanium. So, a titanium rod is implanted into what remains of a patient's bone, extending a small way out of the amputated limb. Then a high-tech robotic prosthesis is clipped on with an 'adapter'.

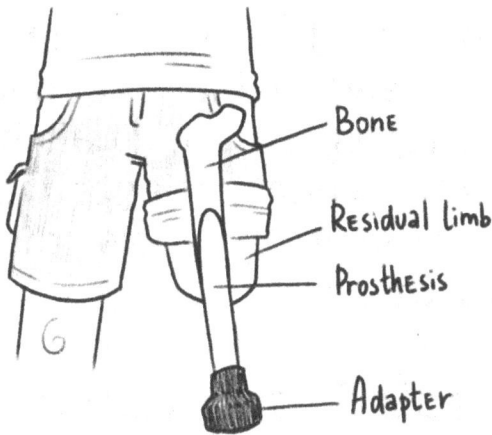

This revolutionary procedure gives amputees not only the ability to walk again but also the sensation of *feeling* themselves walking. Before osseointegration, prostheses had not changed much since the days of pirates wearing a peg leg. For centuries the traditional technique involved simply fitting a socket over a stump. This is uncomfortable for many people and dangerous, as amputees never know where their foot is until it lands on a surface.

With a robotic leg patients have much better control. Their own muscles and nerves redevelop, *integrating* with the titanium. Amputees can feel their new foot before it touches the ground. They also receive better feedback from different surfaces, so their gait becomes more natural. When patients wear long pants it's difficult to know they even have a prosthesis!

Munjed's Osseointegration Specialist Team

- anaesthetists to ensure operations run smoothly
- nurses
- orthopaedic fellows
- pain management specialists
- psychologists to look after mental health
- physiotherapists for rehabilitation
- biomedical engineers
- prosthetists
- peri-operative care managers
- rehabilitation experts
- an amputee representative

Munjed's team of medical specialists share his vision. They work together as an integrated unit to reach the best outcome for each patient.

The team's work in osseointegration gives patients their life back. Knowing this brings Munjed great joy. He takes on even the most challenging cases.

The first Australian osseointegration patient was the sportsman, Brendan Burkett. Brendan's dreams of a career in rugby were shattered in 1985 when a car hit his motorbike. Brendan's pelvis was fractured in three places. One leg was broken in thirteen places and needed to be amputated. Despite these challenges Brendan represented Australia and won medals at many sporting events. In 2000, soon after Munjed left Curtin Detention Centre, Brendan was the Australian flag bearer at the Sydney Paralympic Games.

Ten years later Brendan contacts Munjed. He's a perfect candidate for the new operation. As Munjed prepares Brendon's remaining limb for surgery, he reflects on Brendan's courage and is determined to give him more independence. Brendan's willpower surprises even Munjed and after two operations, this brave sportsman leaves hospital with a walking stick. Only three weeks later, he walks entirely on his own.

Munjed's next patient is Mitch Grant. Mitch's body was smashed in a motorbike accident. His left leg had to be amputated above the knee and he had injuries to his right leg and left arm. After 28 operations, Mitch still has constant pain whenever his suction prosthetic shrinks and swells, and doesn't want more surgery.

But his mother works at the same hospital as Munjed and she keeps raving about his miracle surgical techniques. Eventually Mitch agrees to meet the surgeon just to keep his mum happy. After he has the osseointegration operation, Mitch is surprised how easily he can walk.

Munjed's third patient is Steve Borton, an Australian soldier whose leg was blown off by a landmine in Africa. He is thrilled to be able to walk and live a normal life after his operation.

The success of these operations brings more patients. Soon Munjed becomes one of the country's most respected orthopaedic surgeons and his work makes Australia the place for the world's best osseointegration treatment. Dozens of medical highlights follow, including meeting Queen Elizabeth with a patient and having Prince Harry visit his practice.

Munjed becomes a clinical professor and a world leader of osseointegration treatment. Besides being a great surgeon, Munjed is a compassionate doctor. People ask, what's the secret to his bedside manner? It's simple: he treats patients as human beings, not like a number. He knows what *that* feels like!

***

In early 2017 Munjed receives a phone call. It's an Iraqi voice speaking in Arabic.

'Will you take a call from the Iraqi Prime Minister?'

'Yes, of course,' Munjed replies, trying to hide his surprise.

The Iraqi Prime Minister is inviting him to return to the country of his birth.

'We have thousands of soldiers who have lost limbs in the battle against ISIS,' the Prime Minister's representative says. 'Would you consider coming back to perform osseointegration on some of our amputees?'

Munjed remembers the desperate amputees from his childhood. All those people he'd hoped to help. Never in his wildest dreams could Munjed have imagined returning to Iraq. He's a proud Australian with few personal ties to Iraq, and he's still wary of what could happen in his home country, but the request triggers a sense of duty. Those injured soldiers need him.

13

'I'll be back'

Munjed shivers as the Boeing 737 descends through the dark sky into Baghdad. After almost 20 years he's returning to his childhood home, the place where his father died and the place that he fled 18 years earlier. As the city lights come into view, memories fill his mind. He pinches his nose to steady his breathing and thinks, *what am I doing here?*

In May 2017, Baghdad is one of the most dangerous places on earth. The police can't keep control. Nor can the American soldiers stationed there.

Munjed never thought he'd return and yet here he is.

As the wheels touch down, Munjed remembers the Terminator's words and he laughs.

'*I'll be back...*'

Munjed and his medical team are met by Mohammed, a charming, fashionably dressed representative of the Iraqi Prime Minister.

'Welcome back to your home country,' he says. 'We are honoured to have you here.'

Munjed appreciates Mohammed's kind words, but he feels like an outsider in a strange country. There is no sense of coming home. Munjed feels Australian now.

Two stretch limos and several bodyguards are waiting to take them to the terminal's VIP reception area. There they meet Adam Baidawi, an Australian journalist, who is writing a story about their trip for *The New York Times.* The team transfer into a heavily reinforced four-wheel drive with tinted windows and equipment that can jam remotely triggered IEDs. Munjed feels as if he is in a James Bond movie.

IED stands for **Improvised Explosive Device.** They are made outside of government control and so cannot be regulated. They kill thousands every year in many war-torn countries.

Their four-wheel-drive vehicle is escorted by personnel carrier tanks armed with machine guns. After a short trip along a six-lane highway they arrive at the Prime Minister's luxurious guest house. From there it's another five minutes to the Ibn Sina Hospital.

News of Munjed's visit has spread across the country. When his clinic begins at eight o'clock next morning the hospital corridors and reception area are full. There are patients everywhere. Some have old-style prosthetic legs. Others are in wheelchairs, on crutches or using walking sticks.

Iraq has little support for people with a disability and 40 years of war has created over 150,000 amputees, all desperate for a better life. Most of the patients are ex-soldiers. Just getting to the hospital is a major achievement for them as there is strict security and roadblocks everywhere. Coming inside the hospital is a further challenge. The gates are carefully secured with soldiers in camouflage gear armed with machine guns.

Munjed starts by explaining the osseointegration process to hospital staff. The conference room is packed with surgeons, doctors, nurses and physiotherapists. At nine o'clock the clinic begins. It's mayhem. Badly injured people try to elbow their way to the front. For 15 hours Munjed examines patient after patient. Making improvements in people's lives is Munjed's motivation. It keeps him going. So does coffee.

As he sips a strong Turkish coffee, he remembers his father. If only Abdul Razak Al Muderis could see him now and know that his son never gave up his dreams. Munjed would love to explain how he followed his father's teaching and that making a contribution to society has become his life's work.

More patients arrive the next morning for Munjed's second clinic. Many have travelled for hours. Their stories are all horrific. One is a former soldier, injured after a car bomb explosion. After pulling a boy from the rubble, clasping him to his chest and running to safety, the man was injured by a second explosion. The child's body unintentionally shielded him.

Another patient tackled a suicide bomber. The terrorist detonated his device as the man grabbed him. The terrorist died and Munjed's patient lost both legs. By the end of the clinic Munjed has examined over 90 patients with injuries like this.

'Is that the most people you've seen in such a short time?' Adam, the journalist asks.

Munjed replies, 'I think it's the most anyone has seen in such a short time!'

So many lives have been shattered by the war. Munjed has been invited by the regime with instructions to treat soldiers only, but despairing civilians also swarm the hospital.

'You are not to operate on anyone who is not from the military!' the hospital director shouts.

Munjed reaches their agreed target of 48 soldier operations. Because he has paid all his own expenses for this trip, he is able to insist that he will help civilians too. Munjed knows he can't treat all those who need his skills, but by meeting as many as possible, Munjed wants to give them hope for the future.

During this first trip he identifies 90 potential recipients. In August they begin operating and a plan is made to return four times a year.

Munjed knows education is the best way forward for Iraq. As education levels improve, more people will be able to take steps to repair their country. Over time their goal is to establish a centre of excellence in orthopaedic and trauma surgery. In addition to osseointegration patients, his team replaces hips and takes on complex trauma patients. During this trip, they're able to help 51 patients.

When Munjed and his team return in December 2017, they perform 190 operations, and more surgeries in 2018. All of these trips and the operations are paid for by Munjed himself.

Someone asks him, 'Are you an Iraqi doing this for the people of Iraq?'

'No,' Munjed replies. 'I am an Australian who's coming here to help because I care about you and the country.'

***

Despite the challenges and corruption, Munjed's team feels that they *can* help. Patient by patient and trainee doctor by doctor, they generate hope. And not everything has been destroyed by the conflict. The Iraqi food is as delicious as ever. Munjed enjoys lamb and okra stew, fresh figs and deliciously tart pomegranate juice. Best of all he delights in eating his favourite breakfast, *Gaymer* and *Kahi.*

Some patients' stories stay with Munjed more than others. People like Haithem, the first Iraqi to walk on a robotic leg after osseointegration surgery. Haithem suffered terrible injuries while fighting with the paramilitary. He stood on an IED and the lower half of his right leg was blown off. After medical treatment Haithem was confined to a wheelchair. He tried using a socket prosthesis, but it was too unwieldy. When he left hospital after osseointegration Haithem's goal was to dance again. And he did.

Another patient Munjed will never forget is Armani, a girl who lost both legs when she was ten years old. Munjed meets Armani on his first trip to Baghdad. Her family cannot afford to pay for titanium rods and robotic legs.

'Don't worry,' Munjed says. 'If necessary, I will pay for the implants myself.'

Armani was outside her family home when a mortar shell hit a car. It became a fireball, sending out shockwaves and dislodging a kerosene heater which rolled onto the girl. She suffered horrific burns to her body and lower legs.

Armani was flown to a US Army hospital where she was unconscious for three months. Gangrene set in and after six months both of Armani's legs were amputated below the knees. She lost the will to live, refusing to see family members or her old friends until her mother enrolled her in a group for similar girls. A coach trained her in wheelchair javelin and at the age of 13,

Armani won the first competition she entered. She became the Iraqi age-group javelin champion and won gold medals as a para-athlete at competitions across Asia.

Then she saw an online video about osseointegration...

In 2017 Munjed starts treating Armani. The authorities do not want him to waste time operating on civilians. To them Armani is a no one, but to a doctor and humanitarian, Armani's worth as a child of the world is invaluable. By April 2018 she begins weight-bearing.

'Please lean forward,' Armani asks Munjed from her hospital bed, one day.

'Why?'

Armani smiles and places one of her heavy gold sports medals around his neck.

***

'Thank you,' she says. 'You have given me something precious and I want to do the same. This is for you.'

***

Munjed remembers this moment as he boards the Airbus to begin the long journey home. He watches Baghdad grow smaller and leans back in his seat, picturing an eight-year-old boy zooming his toy plane onto a folding tray table. Then he thinks about the terrifying journey from his Baghdad home, through Jordan, Malaysia, Indonesia, Christmas Island and on to the hellhole of Curtin Detention Centre. Despite the obstacles people have put in his path and the turning wheel of fortune, life has not broken him.

Sometimes people ask, 'What's life about?'

For Munjed, life is about making a difference. We all have a mission in life, he thinks, to leave behind *knowledge* or *charity* that people can live on, or a *legacy* in his children and people he teaches that can carry the mission forward. He hopes he has done all three.

Australia is now the world leader in osseointegration and his patients are trailblazers. They're able to live life more fully and go on to leave their own individual legacies. He thinks about some of his patients who wear out their prostheses too quickly, which motivates him to keep setting new goals.

As the plane gains altitude, Munjed smiles. There is still so much more to be done.

***

Munjed never forgot the small acts of kindness that have shaped his life and his values: a man giving out free ice cream during the Gulf War, the fellow who risked his job so that Munjed could ring his mother from Christmas Island and the guard who helped Munjed make a call from Curtin Detention Centre. At the time, he vowed to pass those kindnesses on when he could.

Now, after all that hard work, even studying for days and months in the hot and horrible detention centre, he has a job where he can truly make a difference with his surgical breakthroughs that are helping people around the world.

His ongoing success demonstrates the valuable contribution so many of our refugees make in Australia.

Munjed's work embodies this, and is formally recognised, when in 2020 he becomes the NSW Australian of the

Year. He is proud of his ancestry *and* proud to be Australian.

Glossary

- **Asylum seeker:** person who has fled their home country and is seeking protection in another.
- **Cyborg:** a being with both organic and electronic body parts – some famous cyborgs you might know include Darth Vader, Tony Stark/Iron Man, and many Terminators.
- **Fundamentalist:** someone who strictly believes in the literal interpretation of religious texts.
- **LGA:** stands for Land Grid Array – a chip socket with pins that you place the main processor on to form a connection.
- **Orthopaedic surgeon:** specialises in diagnosing, treating, preventing and rehabilitating injuries and diseases of the bones, joints, ligaments, tendons and muscles.
- **Osseointegration:** a direct connection between living bone and an artificial limb. A metal titanium implant provides the connection.

- **Prosthesis:** artificial part that replaces a missing part of the body – this could be a limb, a tooth, or even an organ.
- **PTSD:** stands for Post Traumatic Stress Disorder, a mental health condition that's usually triggered by experiencing or witnessing a terrible event. Symptoms include nightmares, flashbacks and anxiety.
- **Refugee:** person who has been forced to leave their country in order to escape war, persecution, or natural disaster.
- **SCUD missile:** a type of powerful tactical missile used in combat since the 1970s, mostly in wars in the Middle East.
- **Speak and Spell machine:** electronic hand-held computer, popular in the 1980s, where you could learn how to spell words by interacting with the machine.
- **Surface-to-air missile (SAM):** a missile launched from the ground to attack and destroy aircraft or other missiles.

- **Surgical registrar:** middle-ranking hospital doctor undergoing training as a specialist.

About Dianne Wolfer

Dianne Wolfer grew up in outer Melbourne, where she made tree-houses and imagined she was Silky from *The Magic Faraway Tree.* Other days she was the Muddle-headed Wombat. When she was ten, Dianne moved to Bangkok with her family for two years. After returning to Australia, she studied at Albury High School and then at Melbourne State Teachers' College. After graduating, she backpacked through Asia and taught children in remote western Nepal.

Dianne's award-winning books have been published in China, Japan, Poland, USA and made into stage plays. She is a bookworm who reads every day. She especially loves animal stories and spent five years researching animal characters in children's literature for her PhD.

Inspiring kindness and imaginative thinking is Dianne's life work.

* 9 7 8 0 3 6 9 3 8 7 5 8 5 *